Kids' **TRAVEL GUIDE** to the **Parables**

Group
Loveland, Colorado
group.com

Group resources really work!

This Group resource incorporates our R.E.A.L. approach to ministry. It reinforces a growing friendship with Jesus, encourages long-term learning, and results in life transformation, because it's

Relational
Learner-to-learner interaction enhances learning and builds Christian friendships.

Experiential
What learners experience through discussion and action sticks with them up to 9 times longer than what they simply hear or read.

Applicable
The aim of Christian education is to equip learners to be both hearers and doers of God's Word.

Learner-based
Learners understand and retain more when the learning process takes into consideration how they learn best.

Kids' Travel Guide to the Parables

Visit our website: **group.com**

Credits
Contributing Authors: Jody Brolsma, Mikal Keefer, Jan Kershner, and Toby Rowe
Cover and Illustrations: Gary LaCoste

Unless otherwise indicated, all Scripture quotations are taken from the *Holy Bible,* New Living Translation, copyright © 1996, 2004, 2007. Used by permission of Tyndale House Publishers, Inc. Carol Stream, Illinois 60188. All rights reserved.

Library of Congress Cataloging-in-Publication Data
Kids' travel guide to the parables / [contributing authors, Jody Brolsma et al. ; cover and illustrations, Gary LaCoste].
    p. cm.
ISBN 978-0-7644-7013-4 (pbk. : alk. paper)
1. Jesus Christ--Parables--Study and teaching. 2. Christian education of children. I. Brolsma, Jody. II. LaCoste, Gary.
BT377.K54 2011
226.809' 505--dc23

2011027930

ISBN 978-0-7644-7013-4

10 9 8 7   18 17 16

Printed in the United States of America.

Kids'
Travel
Guide

Table of Contents

An Introduction to the Travel Guide

Children love stories. So do adults. And in Jesus' parables, we find stories that are much, much more than mere fiction. For millennia, the parables of Jesus have inspired, perplexed, and motivated his followers. On one level, the parables of Jesus are about simple, common things such as mustard seeds and lost sheep. But on another level, they are vividly strange and unpredictable. And unlike fairy tales, parables have no "happily ever after" conclusion. On still another level, they turn the world on its head.

Invite children to go on a journey with you through the parables. Like the parables themselves, the 13 journeys in this book will surprise, comfort, and challenge your children. We hope that they will transform both you and your kids to be more like Jesus.

Kids' Travel Guide to the Parables is designed to be applicable to kids from kindergarten through fifth grade. The lessons explore some of the "greatest hits" of the parables of Jesus, from the more familiar ones such as the Good Samaritan and Prodigal Son, to lesser known ones, such as the Tower Builder and the Persistent Widow.

During this 13-week journey, each child will complete a **Travel Journal**. The Travel Journal will serve as a keepsake so kids can continue to remember the concepts of the parables.

The **Pathway Point** is the central concept that children will explore and apply to their lives. The **Summary of Parable** helps teachers get a quick review of the focus of the parable. A **Travel Itinerary** introduces the lesson and explains how the lesson will impact children's lives.

Please read each lesson thoroughly, and make a model for the crafts before class. If you do, your lessons will flow much more smoothly. The time recommendations are only guidelines. They'll change according to how many are in your group, how prepared you are, and how much help you have. Choose activities or adapt them based on the size of your group and the time you have during your class.

Each lesson starts with a **Departure Prayer**. These are creative prayer activities that help introduce the topic and focus children on God. **Tour Guide Tips** are helps for the teacher, and **Scenic Routes** provide additional creative options.

First Stop Discoveries introduce the children to the lesson's topic. The **Story Excursions** dive deeper into the teachings of the parable. Kids will experience the Bible in creative and varied ways. Choose what you think will best meet

your children's needs. The activities in **Adventures in Growing** lead the children into further application of the Pathway Point. Each week, ask the children if they had opportunities to demonstrate the previous week's Pathway Point in their lives. This will be an important faith-growing time.

Souvenirs are photocopiable paper activities. Have children collect these and keep them in a notebook or folder. When your study on the parables is complete, each child will have a Travel Journal keepsake to use as a reminder of all he or she has learned. Each lesson closes with a **Home Again Prayer**, which offers a time of commitment and a time to ask God to direct kids' lives.

Anytime during your lesson, read the **Fun Facts** section to the kids. These provide examples of the lesson's point with familiar and not-so-familiar facts.

May this exploration of Jesus' parables bring you and the children to a deeper realization of God's great love for you. May these journeys, like the parables themselves, transform you into the kind of person imagined by the Author of the most amazing stories ever told.

The Parable of the Yeast

Pathway Point: 🌑 God grows his kingdom in amazing ways.

> **Summary of Parable:** "Jesus also used this illustration: 'The kingdom of heaven is like the yeast a woman used in making bread. Even though she put only a little yeast in three measures of flour, it permeated every part of the dough.' " (Matthew 13:33)

Travel Itinerary

Today's parable is just one verse—but it's packed with meaning.

Jesus' audience at the time must have been surprised to hear him compare leaven (translated as *yeast* in the New Living Translation) to the kingdom of God. Usually leaven was used as a symbol of wickedness. Even Jesus used the image of yeast in this way (see Matthew 16:6 and Mark 8:15).

But here, in this brief parable, yeast represents something else: the remarkable way the kingdom of God can transform the world.

Jesus' message was one of hope to a small group of people who were already experiencing resistance and criticism (see Matthew 9:33-34 and 12:1-2), a small group that was expected to grow God's kingdom on earth.

Yeast is powerful and alive. And once it begins working in a measure of bread dough, it spreads. It causes the loaf to rise.

That's the transforming power of the kingdom. In the world, certainly, but also in you—and the children you serve.

Let today's lesson be a message of hope for you, too.

Whatever you're facing in life this week, let God's love draw you closer to him. And as you let the kingdom of God grow in you, feel yourself lifted up.

TOUR GUIDE TIP The experiences in this book have been designed for multi-age groups. Select from the experiences, or adapt them as needed for your kids.

DEPARTURE PRAYER

(up to 5 minutes)

In this "yeasty prayer," children will discover that God grows his kingdom in amazing ways.

Say: **Here's something you may've never seen: yeast. In the Bible, the people made leaven, which was a mixture of flour and water that contains yeast—which causes the mixture to rise.**

If you've ever seen someone bake a loaf of bread, you've probably seen them add either leaven or a packet of yeast to the bread dough.

Items to Pack:
¼ cup hot tap water, clear glass 1-cup measuring cup, 1 teaspoon sugar, spoon, small plate, 2 packages of active dry yeast

I'll show you why...but first let's take a look at yeast.

Open a packet of yeast and place it on a small plate.

Place the plate where children can gather around and see and touch the yeast.

Say: **Yeast looks like sand, doesn't it? But it's not—it's actually alive.** Feign sudden worry.

So be careful! It might bite!

Actually, no—it can't bite. No teeth. But it is alive as I'll demonstrate.

Place a quarter-cup of hot tap water into a 1-cup measuring cup. Stir in a teaspoon of sugar. Keep stirring until the sugar is dissolved. Then stir in one package of active dry yeast. Place the cup where it's visible but won't interfere with your prayer time.

Say: **We'll let this set for 10 or 15 minutes, and then check back. If the yeast is alive, it should be doing something by then: It should be growing.**

That's what most living things do: They grow.

You certainly have! Not too many years ago, you were little babies. Now you're...well, you're getting closer to being grown-ups.

Growth is one sign that something is alive and healthy. That's true for our bodies and it's true for the kingdom of God. Jesus started with just a few followers thousands of years ago and now there are millions of followers. The church, if it's healthy, should be growing.

And if we're healthy as people who know and follow Jesus, we should be growing, too—growing stronger and deeper in our faith.

Let's take a few moments and ask God to help us do that today as we look at a story Jesus told.

I'll start by asking God to be with us. If you'd like to, pray with me, and then I'll close for us.

Pray: **God,**

Thank you for giving us life. We want to grow in lots of ways.

Help us grow in our faith. In knowing you better. In following you more closely every day.

Please hear our prayers...

Pause, allowing children time to speak up. Allow 15 to 20 seconds after the last child prays before closing.

Pray: **Thank you, God. In Jesus' name, amen.**

Say: **By the way, I was serious when I said yeast is alive. It's a**

TOUR GUIDE TIP

If you have a small group, gather children around a table and delegate the tasks of stirring and mixing to them.

FUN FACT

In Jesus' day leaven was usually introduced to a fresh batch of bread dough by adding a piece of fermented dough from an earlier loaf.

one-celled member of the fungus family. Add water to yeast, give it some sugar for food, and soon it's happily "burping" carbon dioxide—which is what causes bread to be fluffy.

Let's check back with our yeast experiment in a few minutes to see if burping has commenced!

(15 minutes)

Grow Taller

In this experience, kids will discover that sometimes we need help to grow.

Ask kids to sit together in a circle.

Say: **Let's see if you can remember growing up. I want you to think back—*way* back to your earliest memories.**

For me, one of my earliest memories is...

Briefly share one of your earliest memories.

Say: **Now it's your turn. Tell about one of your earliest memories.**

After several children share, continue.

Say: **Thanks for sharing your memories. It's obvious that you've been growing—and that's a good thing! By the way, how's our yeast doing?**

As a group, examine the mixture. Once the yeast begins to process the sugar, you'll see foam begin.

Say: **Let's make a list: I'd like to know what someone needs to grow. What would you put on our list?**

Expect to hear *food, water, love, encouragement*...probe to see if you can get up to 10 items on your list. Children will quickly mention physical things; prompt them to also include emotional, mental, spiritual, and social necessities for someone to grow.

Say: **Thanks for your ideas. Now let's talk about this...**

Ask: • **What would happen if someone didn't have the items on our list?**

• **Why is it a good thing to keep on growing?**

Say: **You know, one thing that helps us grow is to have others in our lives who are helping us grow.**

When you were very young, you couldn't take care of yourselves. You needed help.

Even now, if you want to grow in your friendship skills, it helps

Nobody could buy yeast in packets in Jesus' day, but yeast spores occur naturally. Those who wished to make raised bread simply mixed flour and water and left it where spores could land. That "sour dough starter" could be added to bread. People still do this today!

Items to Pack:
Bible

When you share appropriately from your life, your kids get to know you. You draw them into the lesson. And you model the sort of response you hope to hear from them.

to have a friend. If you want to become a better soccer player, it helps to be on a soccer team with others.

The Bible says this about growing in our faith and in the kingdom of God...

Read aloud Hebrews 10:24-25.

"Let us think of ways to motivate one another to acts of love and good works. And let us not neglect our meeting together, as some people do, but encourage one another..."

Say: **We can help each other grow. Let's try that now in a game I call Grow Taller. But first: how's our yeast coming along?**

As a group, check the progress of the yeast. By now you should see some foaming as carbon dioxide is released. If not, check back when indicated later.

Have children sit on the floor. Then have them plant their feet on the floor while still sitting. Now ask them to stand without using their hands. Some might be able to stand, but some will not.

Then have children form pairs, if possible with another child about the same size. Age doesn't matter; at issue is body size—you want children about the same size working together.

TOUR GUIDE TIP

If you have more than a dozen children, have children share in pairs or trios. If children are willing, every child should have the chance to talk—that's hard to have happen in a large group.

Say: **Please sit on the floor, back-to-back with your partner. Scoot around so your backs are touching.**

Pause as kids get into position.

Say: **Now plant your feet flat on the floor and reach back so you can lock your arms with your partner.**

Pause as kids get into position.

Say: **Now stand up, pushing against each other. And when you've accomplished that, sit back down again.**

Allow time for children to try this activity. Applaud all efforts.

Say: **Go ahead and unlock from your partner.**

Ask: • **What made it easy or difficult to grow taller with your partner?**

• **How much more difficult was it to try growing taller on your own?**

Say: **Maybe this worked for you and your partner and maybe it didn't...but without your partner you'd have certainly failed to grow taller in this way. We need others to help us grow in our faith—we need God and we need his people.**

But good news: God grows his kingdom in amazing ways. And one of those ways is by helping us grow taller in our faith!

(10 minutes)

I 'Knead' a Workout

Kids will act out making bread, and in so doing discover that God's kingdom grows like leaven in a batch of bread.

Ask: • **How many of you have made a loaf of bread from scratch? Raise your hands.**

• **How many of you have watched someone else make bread from scratch? Raise your hands.**

• **How many of you think that "from scratch" means you're scratching yourself while making bread?**

Say: **Hmmm...well, I'm thinking that maybe you should give bread-making a try now.**

But first, I need to know what you know about baking.

Ask: • **What is your favorite kind of cookie? of pie?**

• **Tell about someone you know who bakes goodies in the kitchen. What does the person make?**

• **If you were going to make bread, what ingredients would you use?**

Say: **Thanks for sharing your stories and ideas. But I can tell that we *definitely* need to practice bread-making!**

Of course, since we don't have a kitchen or all the stuff needed to make bread, we'll have to do this the hard way—by making imaginary bread.

Please sit on the floor and follow my step-by-step instructions. If you miss a step, your imaginary bread will be an imaginary flop— unfit for imaginary consumption!

First, pour three-quarters of a cup of warm water into a bowl...

Pause as children mime what you said.

Now add some salt, sugar, shortening, and milk to the bowl. Stir it all together.

Pause as children mime what you said.

Mix in a cup of flour. Keep stirring...

Pause as children mime what you said.

And now mix in a second cup of flour. Again—keep stirring. Everyone, scratch your noses...

Pause as children mime what you said.

Items to Pack:
Bible

Now you all have imaginary flour on the end of your noses. You look really funny!

Okay, pull the bread dough out of the bowl and plop it on a bread board. It's time to knead the dough by rolling it around and stretching it and then pushing it into a ball again. Let's do that.

Pause as children mime what you said.

A little harder.

Pause as children mime what you said.

A little harder than that.

Pause as children mime what you said.

Not that hard! You'll have bruised bread!

Okay, keep kneading while I read you a parable that Jesus told people about the kingdom of God.

Jesus was talking about what it takes for the kingdom to grow, and he used an image that most people in that day understood: baking bread.

Here's what he said...

Read aloud Matthew 13:33: **"The kingdom of heaven is like the yeast a woman used in making bread. Even though she put only a little yeast in three measures of flour, it permeated every part of the dough."**

Keep kneading!

Back in the day, people kept a piece of dough with yeast in it from yesterday's baking and worked it into today's dough. That way, the yeast could spread and cause the entire loaf of bread to rise.

Point to the foaming yeast in the cup.

Leaven is the lump of dough with yeast in it. Just a bit of that leaven would cause a large loaf of bread dough to rise—in amazing ways.

And ◗God grows his kingdom in amazing ways, too. That's something we'll talk about when we finish our baking.

Okay, kneading is done. Take a quick break and shake out your arms to relax those kneading muscles.

Pause as children shake their arms.

Now, preheat your oven to 375 degrees by turning a dial...

Pause as children mime what you said.

And put the dough in a bowl...

Pause as children mime what you said.

And cover the dough with a towel...

Pause as children mime what you said.

And wait half an hour for the yeast to work and make the bread rise...

Pause and look bored. Check your wrist watch a few times a time or two and then declare a half hour has passed. (No wrist watch? Check your wrist...there's nothing wrong with checking an imaginary watch to time imaginary bread!)

Say: **Now punch down the loaf and knead it again. Okay—stop! No need to knead too much!**

Now the dough goes into the oven, you wait 45 minutes, and presto: fresh bread! Great job! Let's enjoy it now!

ADVENTURES IN GROWING

(15 minutes)

Food for Thought

Children will enjoy fresh bread (from a home or bakery) with butter on it.

Serve children slices of buttered bread on paper towels.

Have small glasses of water available for children, too.

As children eat, ask them to discuss the following:

Ask: • **What do you think the point of Jesus' story was?**

• **What do you think "the kingdom of God" means?**

• **Why do you think it matters whether or not the kingdom of God is growing?**

• **If Jesus wants people to like him and Jesus is all-powerful, why doesn't he just make people like him and join his kingdom?**

Ask for volunteers to collect the paper towels and water glasses and clear them away.

Say: **Usually when you're in a kingdom, you don't have any choice. If you're born in England, you're a subject of the queen or king. That's not how it works in the kingdom of God, though.**

God is looking for volunteers—for people who *want* to be in his kingdom and who will grow when they come.

If you want to grow as someone who knows, loves, and follows Jesus, what can you do to help that happen? How do you—as a person—grow in the kingdom?

Let's talk about that.

Ask: • **How do you—as a person—grow in the kingdom of God? What helps that happen?**

Items to Pack:

fresh bread (as close to homemade as possible), butter, plastic knives, paper towels, small cups of water

(Arrange to warm the bread slices just before serving them—it will add to the image of the bread being fresh out of the oven.)

For extra impact, make bread for this activity using the "Mouth-Watering Bread Recipe" on page 119.

TOUR GUIDE TIP

Substitute gluten-free bread with honey as the snack if gluten or dairy allergies are a concern.

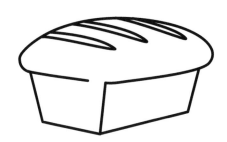

After kids have a chance to brainstorm some ideas, continue.

Say: **Great ideas! Thank you for sharing them.**

Ask: • **Here's another question for you: Are you actually doing those things you suggested? And, if so, what difference is it making?**

Say: ⬤**God grows his kingdom in amazing ways. And God wants to see his kingdom grow wide—with more and more people knowing and loving him—and also for the kingdom to grow deep.**

God wants us to know him better. God wants us to be closer to him.

Deep and wide—that's how God wants to grow his kingdom.

Please get with your back-to-back partner again, but this time, sit facing each other.

Pause as children move.

Say: **In the next few minutes, I'd like you to talk about this...**

Ask: • **What's one way you can help the kingdom of God grow wider? What's one way you can help spread the good news about Jesus to others this week? Be specific—talk about who you want to tell about Jesus, why you picked that person, and how you want to do it.**

You'll have two minutes to talk, so take your time.

Ask: • **How might God want to use you to help the kingdom of God grow wider this week?**

Pause two minutes, and then continue.

Say: **God also wants the kingdom of God to grow deeper. He wants to see us grow in our faith. This week, what would you like to do to help that happen? We had some great ideas, but they won't change our hearts if we don't do them.**

Again, you've got a minute each to talk about what you'd like to do. Pick one thing—something you can do and that you can finish this week. What is it? Tell your partner.

Ask: • **How will you help the kingdom of God grow deeper this week—in you?**

Pause two minutes; then continue.

Say: **Thank you. Deep and wide—that's how the kingdom of God can grow this week. And you'll be a part of it!**

Please let me pray for you.

Pray: **God,**

Thanks for your kingdom and for inviting us to be a part of it. I'm so glad my friends have decided to take you up on your

invitation. They're precious to me and I know you love them.

If someone here hasn't decided to know and love you, please help that person feel your love and decide to be yours.

And I ask that your Holy Spirit bubble up in us and empower us to do the things we've been talking about just now...for your glory.

In Jesus' name, amen.

SOUVENIRS

(10 minutes)

How Am I Growing?

Kids will begin their Travel Journals and create their first Souvenir. This activity helps kids discover that the kingdom of God can grow in them.

Items to Pack:
pocket folders (1 per child), pens, pencils, and a copy of the "Spiritual Growth Chart" on page 18 for each child

Distribute one pocket folder to each child, and have kids write their names on the front. These folders will serve as kids' Travel Journals to collect the Souvenir experience in each lesson. Kids will take their journals and Souvenirs home after Lesson 13 to remind them of their journey through Jesus' parables.

Say: **How many of you have a place where your mom or dad keeps track of your growth? Maybe it's in a book, or maybe there are pencil marks on the wall where you've been measured through the years.**

Just like we grow physically, we can grow spiritually. We can grow closer to God...and grow in how well we listen to and obey God. We can grow stronger.

Let's make a spiritual growth chart.

Give each child a copy of the "Spiritual Growth Chart" handout for this session and also a pen or pencil.

Say: **On your page you'll see an outline of someone who is growing spiritually. I can tell the person is growing because of how this person is living.**

Read aloud the behaviors on the sheet.

I'd like you to turn this into a growth chart for you by having you draw on your sheet. If you love God, trace over the heart. If you think you could grow in how much you love God, make the heart on your sheet a little smaller than the one shown. If you love God a lot, draw your heart bigger than the one shown.

If you're serving God, trace over the arms on your sheet. If you could do a better job serving God, make your arms smaller. Serving a lot? Draw big arms!

I'll give you time to draw on your sheet. Let's see how your growth chart turns out.

Allow children time to draw. Then ask children to show their charts to a partner and discuss the following:

Ask: **• Where does my chart show I have room to grow?**

• Where does my chart show I'm growing a lot?

Say: **When we grow closer to God, the kingdom of God is growing.** 🌑 **God grows his kingdom in amazing ways—like in us!**

When God is growing us, it shows in how we live. The closer you get to Jesus, the deeper we grow in the kingdom of God. And the more willing and able we are to share his love with others!

Ask children to return pens and pencils, and place their Spiritual Growth Charts in their Travel Journals.

| **HOME AGAIN PRAYER** | (up to 5 minutes) |

Say: **I'd like you to do something with me now: a posture prayer.**

That means we'll pray together, but we'll change our posture as we move through our prayer together.

I'll lead, but you'll have a chance to pray, too. You can pray out loud or quietly—it's up to you. But please move with me from one position to the next. Our bodies will express our prayers, too.

Please join me in kneeling on the floor to begin.

Pause as children join you kneeling.

I'll begin. Please join me in praying.

Pray: **God, you are good and you are great. You are mighty and marvelous. We kneel before you because you are worthy of our praise.**

Please hear us as we praise you now.

If you'd like to pray out loud, please do so now.

Pause so children can pray.

And now please stand with your hands at your side and your heads bowed. Join me as I pray.

Pray: **God, thank you for your love. We come to you knowing that we don't deserve your love—it's a gift, a free gift, a gift we gladly receive. Please forgive us for the things we've done that are wrong.**

We silently think of those things now. We ask for you to forgive us, for your grace to wash us clean.

Items to Pack:

a copy of the "Mouth-Watering Bread Recipe" handout on page 119 for each child

Pause so children can pray.

Pray: **Thank you, God.**

Now please raise your hands and cup them together in front of you. Join me as I pray.

God, we want what you want. We want to ⬤**see you grow your kingdom in amazing ways. Please use us to help others know about you. And please help us grow into the people you want us to be.**

Hear our prayers as we ask you to use us.

Pause so children can pray.

And now please raise your hands above your heads in a symbol of praise. Join me as I praise God.

Pray: **God, you keep your promises. You are faithful. You are true. We know you've said your kingdom will stand forever and that we can be a part of it. Thank you! We praise you.**

Hear our praises.

Pause so children can praise God.

Pray: **In Jesus' name, amen.**

Say: **I have a lovely parting gift for you: a recipe so you can make real bread at home!**

Distribute the "Mouth-Watering Bread Recipe" take-home handout (p. 119).

Say: **You'll need a mom or dad on duty to help with this because sharp knives and ovens are involved. Hey, you didn't think baking bread was for wimps, did you? This is dangerous, could-burn-down-your-house stuff; not for the weak-hearted!**

Give it a try this week and tell me how it went when you come back next week. And tell me how God used *you* to grow the kingdom deep and wide this week, too!

Spiritual Growth Chart

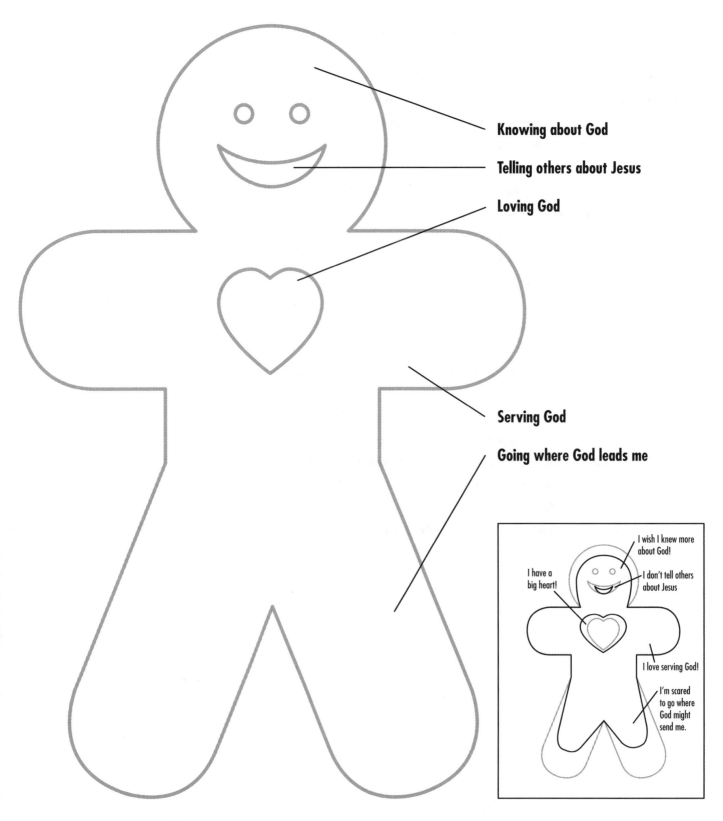

Knowing about God

Telling others about Jesus

Loving God

Serving God

Going where God leads me

I wish I knew more about God!

I have a big heart!

I don't tell others about Jesus

I love serving God!

I'm scared to go where God might send me.

The Parable of the Talents

Pathway Point: God wants us to do our best with the talents he gives us.

> **Summary of Parable:** The master entrusts money (talents) to three servants. Two risk investing; one hides the talent given to him. Upon his return, the master rewards the risk-takers and chastises the servant who played it safe. (Matthew 25:14-30)

Travel Itinerary

Ask a 5-year-old if he or she is an artist...dancer...singer...or runner and you'll hear an enthusiastic "yes."

By the time children are a few years older, they're less sure of their talents. They're comparing themselves with others who are better artists...dancers... singers...or runners. They may be unsure what their talents are—or they may not value what they do easily or well.

In the parable you'll share today, Jesus drives home the point that no matter what you've been given, God expects you to use it for his benefit. Humility is great, but it doesn't excuse us from owning and using our God-given abilities.

So today is a day of discovery for your children...and, perhaps, for you.

Together you'll sort out what God's given you. How to use it to serve others. And how to use those gifts to glorify God.

It'll be an affirming, fun day. Enjoy it!

TOUR GUIDE TIP The experiences in this book have been designed for multi-age groups. Select from the experiences, or adapt them as needed for your kids.

TOUR GUIDE TIP You'll read aloud Matthew 25:14-30 to your children. Practice this out loud at least three times. Get comfortable with the flow of the story. Add inflections to your reading, or a voice for the master. How you *tell* the story will do a great deal to encourage your children to *listen* to it!

Items to Pack:
none

DEPARTURE PRAYER	(up to 5 minutes)
	In this "shape-shifting prayer," children will discover that God has given them skills and gifts they can use to serve others and praise God.

Ask children to stand in the center of the room.

Say: **Right now there are satellites zooming by overhead. Let's imagine that one is directly over us and can look down on us. And since it's equipped with X-ray vision, it's looking through the ceiling. Everyone wave!**

Lead the kids in waving at the ceiling.

Say: **Today we're talking about using our time, talents, and money—**

Yes, there really are satellites hovering overhead, a *lot* of them. According to the Space Surveillance Network, there are about 8,000 objects currently in orbit around planet Earth; about 560 of them are operational satellites.

anything God has given us. Mostly we'll talk about our talents, and I know we have talented people in this room.

I'd like to show whoever is watching from the satellite what talents we have in this room, but the satellite can't hear us. It can only see us—and from straight overhead.

So let's do this: let's use our bodies to squeeze into shapes they can see from above.

For instance, I think we've got some good singers here so let's squeeze into the shape of a microphone. How could we move around so from above we look like a microphone?

Allow time for children to figure out how to move to make the shape.

Say: **Great! What are other talents people here have besides singing?**

Allow children to make suggestions and to also recommend shapes that reflect their talents. If you have a shortage of suggestions, consider these: sports (football shape), writing (pencil shape), and math (book shape). Suggest they figure out what shape will reflect the talents of being a good friend or being kind, too.

Ask children to be seated.

Say: **We've got talented people here in this room!**

Some of our talents are the kinds that end up in the spotlight while others aren't as obvious. Some will be applauded and others won't. But no matter what kind of talent you have—and you *all* have talent—your talent is important because it's a gift from God. And no matter what talents God has given us, God wants us to do our best with the talents he gives us.

Let's make one more shape together: a circle. Please stand and do that.

Pause as kids form a circle.

We're in a circle because our talents are a circle, too. They come from God...and if we're using them to help others and honor him, they return to God, too. Sort of like in a circle everything comes back to the same point.

Let's take a moment and thank God for our talents he's given us. I'll close.

Pause.

After 30 seconds, pray: **Dear God, thank you for giving us talents. Today help us discover what they are and how we can use them to honor you and to help others.**

In Jesus' name, amen.

Items to Pack:
none

(15 minutes)

Stretchers

Kids will discover that, though they may not have everything they want, God expects them to do their best with what they have.

Form your children into groups—four children in a group. If you have a small group, pair kids together. If you have just one child, the two of you will be a team.

Place all groups along one wall in your room.

Say: **Let's play a game I call Stretchers.**

The goal is to use what you have with you to reach from this wall to that far wall—and even back again if you can figure out how to do it.

You need to create one long chain using whatever you have with you. For instance, you could pull out your shoelaces and lay them end to end to make part of your chain. What else do you have with you that you could add to stretch even further? I'll leave that up to you, but work together on your team and work fast—you'll have just four minutes to make your chain.

Ready? Go!

Keep kids posted on the time by announcing when each minute has passed. When four minutes have passed, applaud your kids' efforts and then give them a minute to re-lace their shoes, put back on their belts, and otherwise get reassembled.

Ask them to sit together on the floor. In their groups, have them discuss the following questions.

Ask: • **If you'd known you were going to play this game today, what would you have brought with you from home to help you—and why?**

• If you could carry a special bag with just three items in it—a bag that would help you deal with anything that happened—what would you put in the bag?

• Tell about a time you didn't have what you needed when a problem arose and you had to use what you had with you to fix the problem. What happened? What did you do?

After kids have shared together, say: **Thanks for sharing in your group!**

Please tell the larger group what items you think should be in that "be-ready-for-anything" bag you talked about.

Solicit answers from several children before moving along.

TOUR GUIDE TIP

Ask your kids to lobby for who they think the world's best athlete might be. Then ask if any of them consider themselves to be the world's best athlete. If not, ask if that means they shouldn't be athletes at all. The point: Just because we can't be the "world's best" doesn't mean we can't have fun in sports and other challenges—and be the best us we can be.

FUN FACT

In Jesus' day the term *talent* was used to indicate a weight—especially one used to weigh precious metals. Since we don't know precisely how much silver was in a talent, we don't know how much money each servant got...but it was a lot!

Items to Pack:

Bibles

Say: **Unfortunately, it's hard to have a bag with everything in it from a million dollars to anti-bully spray to a snow-shovel.**

But there *is* a sort of bag that you carry everywhere, and there's something really special and unique in it. It's the bag of your gifts and talents—things that God has given you.

Some of you can sing. Some of you are athletes. Some of you can do math, or read quickly, or you're great at making friends or serving others. But no matter what you can do, that ability is a gift from God. And no matter what your ability, 🕐God wants you to do your best with the talents he gave you.

That's the lesson three servants learned in a story that Jesus told.

Let's take a look at that story—and what it means to us!

STORY EXCURSION

(15 minutes)

Freeze Frame

Kids will create human tableaus portraying moments in a story Jesus told about three servants who were entrusted with their Master's money.

Form children into trios.

Say: **Jesus told a story about his kingdom, and how God wants us to do the best we can with what God gives us. I'll read the story aloud to you.**

Please listen carefully—you'll need to do something with the information!

Read aloud—with feeling—Matthew 25:14-30 to your children.

Please use the New Living Translation or another easy-to-understand version. And rehearse reading this story aloud several times so you can do so smoothly and with inflection in your voice.

After you finish reading, have children discuss the following in their trios:

Ask: • **Which servant reminds you of yourself? Why?**

• **Do you think the Master was too hard on the third servant—the one who hid money in the dirt? Why or why not?**

• **Tell about a time you did—or didn't—do a great job taking care of something for someone. What happened?**

Say: **Thanks for sharing in your trio.**

I have a job for you and your two friends: please create a tableau of one moment in that story.

A tableau is when people look like they were freeze-framed as they were in the middle of doing something. Your job is to pick a moment in the story—whatever moment you want—and pose so the rest of us will be able to guess which moment you've chosen.

Two rules: First, you can't talk or move. Once you're in place, you're *frozen* in place!

And second, all three of you have to be in the scene...even if one of you is just a piece of furniture!

In your trio, pick out a moment you want to capture in your tableau and rehearse. You'll have three minutes to decide on a moment and work out the details, so get busy!

If your trio would like to move to a part of the room where no one can hear your discussion, that's fine—go ahead and do so.

After three minutes, have everyone sit. One at a time, have trios stand up and get in position. Encourage other trios to guess which moment the tableau is portraying—and which child is which character in the story.

Applaud all efforts.

Great job! I've never imagined that parable looking quite like that, but it gave me some new insight. Thank you!

Jesus wanted his audience to learn something: ◗God wants us to do our best with the talents he gives us.

That's a lesson for us, too. Let's talk more about that now.

ADVENTURES IN GROWING

(10 minutes)

Food for Thought

Children will discover that making the most of what they've been given sometimes requires they cooperate with others.

Say: **Let's keep talking about using our talents as we enjoy some snacks!**

Tell children they'll eat in their trios.

First, give each child a few paper towels.

Say: **I've got a treat for each of you. I'll put your treat on your paper towel, but don't touch what I give you. Just leave it on your paper.**

In each trio give the first child three plastic knives, the second child a short stack (six) of crackers, and the third child a blob of icing.

Remind kids to not touch the items on their paper towels, and then discuss the following:

Tableau: short for the French term *tableau vivant* (literally: *living picture*) in which a group of silent and motionless participants portray a scene.

Items to Pack:
wheat and/or gluten-free crackers, paper towels, plastic knives, icing

TOUR GUIDE TIP

Substitute honey for icing if your there are allergy concerns or if your church has a wellness policy regarding sweets.

Ask: • **Would you like to exchange your individual snack item for someone else's snack item? Why or why not?**

• **What would happen if you combined what you have with what the rest of your trio has? What snack might you make?**

Say: **Actually, combining your stuff sounds like a good idea. Do that while I tell you about something that happened to me.**

Share with your kids a brief story about a time you were part of a team...a group that could do something as a team that you couldn't have done alone.

For instance, perhaps your soccer team won a game you could never have won by yourself. Or you and a friend worked together on a school project and by combining your talents you had a better outcome.

When you've finished sharing, continue.

Say: **When you shared what you had on your paper towel with your trio, you ended up with a better snack than you'd have had on your own.**

Our talents work like that.

When we bring our talents together, we can accomplish things we could never do alone.

Ask: • **Tell about a time you were part of a team that accomplished something you couldn't have done alone. What did your team do— and what did you contribute to the effort?**

After children share, continue.

Say: **Thanks for sharing your stories.**

God has given us all one or more talents we can use to honor him and help others. And **God wants us to do our best with the talents he gives us.**

Let's figure out what our talents are now...but first, please work together in cleaning up and getting rid of the trash.

Pause as kids collect the trash and dispose of it.

Keep icing distribution fair by using a small ice cream scooper to put a scoop of icing on paper towels.

When you share an appropriate story from your life, your kids get to know you. And you signal the discussion is relevant— because it's relevant to *your* life, too.

SOUVENIRS

(10 minutes)

I Like...

This activity helps children discover the talents God has given them.

Items to Pack:
Bible, a pencil and a copy of the "I Like..." handout on page 27 for each child

Say: **Sometimes the talents God gives us aren't the kind we can show off on stage. Maybe we can't sing, but we can serve others. Maybe we can't juggle, but we can be joyful.**

In fact, I *guarantee* that God wants to give you some special talents that will change you—from the inside out!

Read aloud Galatians 5:22-23 from the Bible:

"But the Holy Spirit produces this kind of fruit in our lives: love, joy, peace, patience, kindness, goodness, faithfulness, gentleness, and self-control. There is no law against these things!"

Say: **When you know, love, and follow Jesus, the Holy Spirit begins building those character traits in you. You begin to grow in those special areas...really!**

Form kids into pairs.

Ask: • **Tell about a time God helped you be kind to someone. Who was it? What happened? Tell your partner.**

• **Would you rather be joyful or amazingly good at playing a musical instrument? Why?**

Thank kids for sharing with their partners.

Say: **Good news! You can be really good as a musician *and* be joyful! Let's take a little test to see what our God-given talents might be.**

Give each child an "I Like..." handout. If you have younger children who are beginning readers, pair them with older children who can help walk their younger partners through the handout.

Say: **Maybe you like all eight of the things on your handout. But pick the three you like *most* and circle them with your pencil.**

Pause as children decide what to circle.

Say: **Often, our talents line up with things we enjoy, things we do easily and well. Find a partner and discuss this:**

Ask: • **Show your partner what you circled. What do you enjoy about those three areas you circled?**

• **What do you do in those areas that you find fun?**

Say: **Maybe those things you do well are your God-given talents!**

TOUR GUIDE TIP

If you have a small group, it's okay to have children talk as a group. The goal is for each child to talk—that's when self-discovery seems to happen best.

Items to Pack:

pencils and "I Like..." handouts from previous activity

If so, 🌑 **God wants you to do your best with the talents he gave you.**

On your handout you'll see ways you can use your skills and talents to serve others.

Talk with your partner about this:

Ask: • **How have you used your skills and talents to help others?**

• **What's a way to help others that you may not have tried yet? Maybe your partner has some ideas for you!**

God also gives us talents so we can honor him. How might you use your skills and talents to do that? to help at church?

HOME AGAIN PRAYER (up to 5 minutes)

Ask children to find partners.

Say: **It's easy to sometimes feel like we don't have any talents, that God skipped us when he was handing them out. But trust me: You have skills...and you don't have to wait until you're a grown-up to use them to help others and honor God.** 🌑**You can do your best with the talents God has given you—right now!**

Please give your "I Like..." handout to your partner.

Pause as children do this.

Say: **Now, please pray for your friend. Ask God to help your friend serve God with his or her talents. Pray quietly and I'll close for us.**

Pause.

Pray: **God, thank you for all the good gifts you give us.**

The gift of this day. Of our friendships. Of your love.

And thank you for the talents that you've planted in us. I can look at these friends and see already how you've given them so much.

May they love and serve you all their lives.

And may they always do their best with the talents you've given them.

In Jesus' name, amen.

Say: **Please take a minute to write or draw an encouraging note or a picture on the back of your friend's "I Like..." handout. Write or draw something positive!**

Allow a minute for children to write or draw and then ask them to return "I Like..." handouts to their owners. They'll immediately review what was written! Have children place the handouts in their Travel Journals.

I LIKE...

MOVING MY BODY
- Play sports with friends
- Do a dance
- Build a gift

MUSIC
- Play an instrument
- Sing a solo
- Write a song

WORDS
- Read to younger kids
- Write a nice note to a friend
- Create a poem

QUIETLY THINKING
- Pray for others
- Keep a prayer journal
- Meditate

OTHER PEOPLE
- Listen
- Make friends
- Share with others

NATURE
- Care for a pet
- Plant a garden
- Hike with a friend

MATH AND SOLVING PROBLEMS
- Help friends with homework
- Plan a party
- Organize a closet

ART
- Draw pictures for friends
- Make a puppet
- Take photographs

The Parable of the Prodigal Son

Pathway Point: God forgives us when we sin.

Summary of Parable: A son outrageously demands his inheritance from his father before the father has died. The father gives it to him. The son leaves and goes to a faraway land, where he quickly squanders the money. The son falls into poverty, and survives by taking care of pigs. The broken son returns home, where his father lovingly welcomes him back with a lavish feast. The other son comes to the house, learns what is going on, and refuses to go into the house. The father goes out to the other son and pleads with him to understand that his brother was lost, but now is found. (Luke 15:11-32)

Travel Itinerary

At first, the kids in your group may have a hard time making the connection of forgiveness from a story that's about being lost and found. *Lost* and *found* are concrete terms for kids. They've all had a favorite toy that's been lost, and then later found. But that doesn't mean that anyone needs forgiving, does it?

So throughout your discussion, help kids understand how the prodigal son got lost from God by choosing to do the wrong thing and wandering away. Unlike a toy, the main character in this story got up and left. He shouldn't have. But when it was time to come back—to become found—his father was eager to forgive and have a relationship with his child. That's God.

God always wants to make today a new day in our lives by forgiving the past and moving forward, by saying, "Welcome home." For kids, the "past" might be a little different than for adults. But they have issues, struggles, and sins like every other person. This adventure will help them understand God's forgiveness through the lens of their own story, whatever that might be, and lead them to share God's love and forgiveness with the people around them.

DEPARTURE PRAYER (up to 5 minutes)

Bring kids together in a circle, and ask:

• **Who here likes going shopping at the toy store?**

Say: **Well today, I have something for you to think about. I'm**

TOUR GUIDE TIP

The experiences in this book have been designed for multi-age groups. Select from the experiences, or adapt them as needed for your kids.

Items to Pack:

a copy of the "Toy Gift Certificate" handout on page 36 for each child

(Optional: Buy your kids $5 gift certificates to a toy store to use in place of the reproducible gift certificate, or to give out as a fun surprise at the end of today's lesson.)

---

going to put something in front of you, but you can't touch it. You can only look at it.

Place Toy Gift Certificates in front of kids on the table or floor one at a time.

Right before your very eyes is $100 worth of toys! Who wants to go spend it right now? Let's pretend for a moment that you could go spend it right now if you want. But here's the catch: If you picked it up and wanted to shop with it right now, you would not be able to return to our group. Ever. In other words, if you took the gift certificate and went toy shopping, you'd be saying goodbye to our group and your friends for good. Done.

However, if you chose to stay, I would recollect the toy money and you would not get to use it at all. So by staying, you'd get to stay with the group and keep your friends, but you'd lose out on the toy money.

Invite kids to pick up the gift certificates and hold them.

Ask: • **So, which do you choose? Take it and leave—or stay and give up the toy money?**

• **If this were more toy money, how would you choose and why?**

• **If this were real money, actual cash...and lots of it, what would you do?**

Say: **Sometimes the idea of having lots of money or lots of stuff can be pretty appealing—especially if it's a LOT of stuff. Sometimes, we even might feel like we'd be better off on our own.**

Ask: • **If you decided to leave your family today and never come back, what do you think you would miss the most?**

Say: **That's what today's Bible story is about. A child who thought he'd have more fun on his own if he could just get enough money from his parents. And he got it—all of it. But what he found out later was that all the money and stuff in the world couldn't replace the relationship he had with his family.**

Let's ask God to help us appreciate the relationships we have with the people in our families, and to also help us understand the rest of today's Bible parable.

Pray: **Dear God, thank you for the people in our families. Help us appreciate those relationships and not let stuff, or money, or something else that seems more fun distract us from loving the people in our lives. In Jesus' name, amen.**

1st STOP DISCOVERY

(15 minutes)

Setting Up Obstacles

Kids will turn the room into an obstacle course that represents the obstacles that we all create in our relationships.

TOUR GUIDE TIP

Ahead of time, be prepared to move your room around. If your room doesn't have lots of moveable objects in it, bring in some. Extra chairs, random items, traffic cones—anything that kids will be able to move around and set up as obstacles. Be mindful of your age group when thinking of appropriate items.

FUN FACT

Actual "pockets" were invented by James L. Pocket in 1698 in South Dakota, in an effort to stop losing loose change. If only they made people-sized pockets!

Gather kids in front of the white board.

Say: **Sometimes we do or say things that we shouldn't do or say. And when we do those things, it makes God sad, and the people around us sad as well. In today's Bible passage, the prodigal son made his father and entire family sad. Here's what happened after he took all of his money and left.**

Here's what the Bible says: **"A few days later this younger son packed all his belongings and moved to a distant land, and there he wasted all his money in wild living. About the time his money ran out, a great famine swept over the land, and he began to starve. He persuaded a local farmer to hire him, and the man sent him into his fields to feed the pigs. The young man became so hungry that even the pods he was feeding the pigs looked good to him. But no one gave him anything"** (Luke 15:13-16).

At this point, the son didn't feel like he could come home.

Ask: • **Why do you think he'd feel that way?**

Say: **When we do wrong things, or say hurtful things, or think thoughts that aren't from God, we create obstacles that get in the way of us having good relationships. Those obstacles make it hard to have good friendships and family relationships, and just make things feel weird. So let's talk about some of those obstacles.**

On the board, write three categories: Small Obstacles, Medium Obstacles, Large Obstacles.

Ask: • **What are some obstacles in your lives? Things that you do wrong, fail to do, thoughts you think that you shouldn't, anything like that.**

Invite kids to give answers. Help them out with an example or two if needed, such as gossiping about a friend at school, yelling at a sibling, taking something that belongs to someone else, and so on. When kids give an answer, ask the group if it is a small, medium, or large obstacle. Get the whole group in on the discussion. Then write the obstacle under the appropriate column on the board. When you've recorded several answers, point to the board.

Say: **Wow! Look at the board. That's a lot of obstacles that we cre-ate in our lives. Obstacles that make it hard to have good, loving rela-tionships with the important people in our lives. Some of these things are obstacles that are pretty hard to forgive.**

Ask: **• Which of these would be the hardest for you to forgive if someone did it to you—and why?**

• How would you feel if someone did all these things to you?

• Why do you think God forgives us for all the obstacles we put in the way of our relationship with him?

Say: **I need your help. We need to set up obstacles in this room for later. Some obstacles can be small, some can be medium, and others can be big. Want to help?** (Get them excited!) **Let's do it!**

Get the whole group helping in moving stuff around. Make it as big and fun as you can tolerate. When your room is a big obstacle course, continue.

Say: **Look at this room! It looks like fun for now. But if this were real life, that would mean that life was a mess. And for the prodigal son, who was away from home, out of money, had no job, and no toys or fun stuff left, life really *was* a mess.**

Kids will get pretty excited during this activity. You may want to give them a safety briefing and set some rules before moving your room around.

STORY EXCURSION

(15 minutes)

Living Water

This experience will teach kids that God wants us to overcome any obstacle to return to him, and will always forgive us when we return.

Items to Pack:
Bibles, a tasty treat for each person, blindfolds for half your group

Gather kids together in the part of the room that feels the most surrounded by obstacles. Open your Bible to Luke 15:11-32, and show kids the passage.

Say: **Before we keep going with the parable of the prodigal son, let's review what's happened so far.** Ask kids to tell what they've learned so far about today's passage.

Then ask kids to form pairs. In their pairs, have them read the next part of the Bible story, Luke 15:17-22. When pairs are finished, get everyone's attention.

Ask: **• In your own words, what happened next?**

• How did you feel about the father's reaction?

• Explain why you'd find it harder to be away from home, or to be at home missing someone you love.

Say: **Today's Bible passage tells us that no matter what obstacles we've set up for ourselves, God always wants us to return to him. God**

Some children have food allergies that can be dangerous. Know your children, and consult with parents about allergies their children may have. Also, read food labels carefully, as hidden ingredients can cause allergy-related problems.

always wants to forgive us and make things right. There's never a time where God won't welcome us and love us. And we're going to experience a little of what that might have been like right now.

In your pairs, pick who will be the "father" and who will be the "son." Don't worry—you'll get a chance to switch later.

Here's how this is going to work. I have [type of tasty treat] for everyone. But you won't get it from me. You'll get it from the father in your pair, after you make it through the obstacle course. Choose a place for your son to start, and then the father will go to the other side of the room across the obstacle course. We'll all do this at once. So the son will call out, "Father, Father!" And the father will call out, "Come home, come home!" Keep going—and be careful—until you cross all the obstacles to get to your father. While you're doing this, remember how the father ran to the son and helped get him home, right? So maybe you fathers can do the same.

Blindfold the sons and line them up along one wall. Give the tasty treats to the fathers. Yes—this will be noisy and rowdy. When one round has finished, invite kids to switch places, get everyone reset, and then play again. When it's all finished, gather the kids in a circle with their treats.

Ask: • **How did it feel to go through the obstacle course blindfolded?**

• **What changed when your father started helping you?**

• **How did some obstacles get in the way more than others?**

• **How is this like coming to God for forgiveness and God giving it to you?**

Say: **Just like this obstacle course was fun, the Bible said that the father was so excited to see his son return that he threw a party. That's the kind of God we love and follow. God is always excited to see you—even if you've made a big mess of things. God forgives us when we sin.**

SCENIC ROUTE → Have the group look back around the room. Ask them how your time together would be different if the obstacles were always there and never went away? Guide the discussion to help them understand that while today might have been crazy-fun, a life filled with constant obstacles would be frustrating and exhausting.

Items to Pack:
Bibles, CD player with up-beat worship music ready to play, foam ball

ADVENTURES IN GROWING

(10 minutes)
Share the Love
Kids will learn to not be like the older brother in the prodigal son story.

Ask the kids sit in a circle. Open your Bible to Luke 15:28-32. Show the kids the Scripture. Read the passage:

"The older brother was angry and wouldn't go in. His father came out and begged him, but he replied, 'All these years I've slaved for you and never once refused to do a single thing you told me to. And in all that time you never gave me even one young goat for a feast with my friends. Yet when this son of yours comes back after squandering your money on prostitutes, you celebrate by killing the fattened calf!' His father said to him, 'Look, dear son, you have always stayed by me, and everything I have is yours. We had to celebrate this happy day. For your brother was dead and has come back to life! He was lost, but now he is found!' "

Ask: • **Explain how you feel about how the older son reacted.**

• **What would you do if your brother or sister did something really, really wrong but didn't get in trouble?**

• **How do you think God expects us to feel when he forgives others, even if their sins are really serious?**

• **How can you show your family members your love and forgiveness this week?**

Say: **God wants us to celebrate with our family members and be happy for them—even when they get something extra special. To do that, sometimes it's best to focus on what's awesome about the people in our family. And we'll get to practice that a little bit right now.**

Explain that when the music starts, you'll pass around a ball. When the music stops, the person with the ball stands in the middle and everyone quickly says a favorite thing about that person. Then that person rejoins the circle. After someone has been in the middle, his or her job is to make sure that the ball quickly gets to another person who hasn't had it yet.

Play the game, giving every person a chance to be in the middle.

Ask: • **Explain what you would have said if your brother was the prodigal son and he was standing in the middle of the circle.**

• **Why is it harder to be frustrated or angry with people after a game like this?**

Say: **Let's open our Bibles to 2 Thessalonians 1:3, and read it all together.** (Allow time for everyone to get there.) **"Dear brothers and sisters, we can't help but thank God for you, because your faith is flourishing and your love for one another is growing."**

Ask: • **What does it mean for something to flourish?**

• **Describe a time when you or someone you know flourished.**

Say: **When you experience God's forgiveness, it makes your heart** softer toward other people. And when you love others—like what we just did in our circle—your heart grows softer toward others. We can start to see others, including people in our own families, the way God sees them. God forgives us when we sin. He wants us to forgive others, too.

Ask: • **How can forgiving and loving someone make your faith grow and flourish?**

Then say: **This next experience will help us remember what we've been learning today.**

SOUVENIRS
→

(10 minutes)

Welcome Home

Kids will make a reminder that God will always forgive them.

Set out "Welcome Home" papers from page 37, markers, crayons, and stickers for decoration, and the aluminum foil and tape.

Say: **Today we're learning that God forgives us when we sin. And no matter what obstacle we've made, no matter what sin we've committed, no matter what wrong thing we've done, God will always welcome us home. Just like what happened in our obstacle course.**

Today, you can make a reminder of an obstacle in your life that God will forgive or has forgiven. It could be something we wrote on the board or something else you've thought of.

Ask: • **What's the biggest thing in your life that you need God's forgiveness for?**

Say: **You don't have to answer out loud. Just think about it. It could be something very specific or very general.**

As you think about your answer, I'd like you consider what your answer might look like if it were right in front of you. I have lots of aluminum foil. It's easy to sculpt, shape, tear, or bunch up to make an object. Take a piece and make an aluminum sculpture of what you just thought about.

When you're finished, come get a Welcome Home sign. You can decorate it, add stickers to it, or do whatever you want to make it fun for you. It folds in half, and you can set it up in your room as a reminder that no matter what, God will forgive you.

Items to Pack:
lots of aluminum foil, tape, copies of "Welcome Home" handout on page 37, markers, crayons, stickers

TOUR GUIDE TIP
Before the lesson, it will be very helpful if you make your own example of an aluminum foil sculpture.

We'll do this part quietly, without talking, because it's between you and God. Have fun.

Encourage kids to be creative. For example, sin could be represented by a big blob of foil, with a cross coming out of it to stand for God's forgiveness. Or anger could be represented by an angry face made out of foil.

When kids are done, continue.

When you get home, set your foil sculpture somewhere special. Then, take your welcome home sign and put it in front of or on top of the sculpture. Every time you see it, remember that no matter what, God wants to ⬤forgive us when we sin, just like in the story of the prodigal son. Before we close, let's take a minute to thank God for what he has taught us today and for forgiving us all the time.

Have kids place their Welcome Home creations in their Travel Journals.

HOME AGAIN PRAYER | (up to 5 minutes)

Say: **Today has been pretty busy and fun. And maybe through all that we've done, you've thought of something you need God's forgiveness for. God wants to forgive you, and he wants you to come to him with anything and everything in your life. I'm going to guide you in some quiet prayer times where you can talk to God. Let's bow our heads.**

Silently thank God for being so forgiving. Pause.

Silently talk to God about something you've done that you need forgiveness for. Pause.

Silently talk to God about forgiving someone else for something he or she has done to you. Ask for God's help in that relationship. Pause.

Silently thank God for your family and friends. Pause.

Silently thank God for his son, Jesus, and that he gave us eternal life.

After a few moments, pray: **God, thanks for giving us such a fun day. Thank you for the story of the prodigal son, and teaching us that no matter what we can always turn back to you, and you'll forgive us and give us a new start. In Jesus' name, amen.**

Gift Certificate

Good for 1 Toy of your choice

Toy for YOU!

for

look!

100 100 100 100

The Parable of the Lost Sheep

Pathway Point: God cares for each of us.

Summary of Parable: A shepherd leaves 99 sheep in the dangerous wilderness to find the one lost one. (Matthew 18:10-14)

Travel Itinerary

Jesus is so amazing, isn't he? The parables he told connected with his audience thousands of years ago, and they connect to us today! What better illustration to show us our worth to him than that of a lost sheep, whose shepherd leaves the flock to come save the wanderer and bring it back into the fold.

The kids in your group may be feeling like lost sheep. They may not say so directly. But kids whose families are splitting up, kids who face bullies at school, kids who don't make friends easily—they're all feeling like lost lambs. They need to know that there's a good shepherd who cares deeply for them—who loves them so much that he laid down his life for them.

And *you* get to tell them about the good shepherd! What a privilege. Use today's adventure as a way to encourage your kids. Use it as a way to help them draw closer and closer to the shepherd who loves them.

TOUR GUIDE TIP

The experiences in this book have been designed for multi-age groups. Select from the experiences, or adapt them as needed for your kids.

DEPARTURE PRAYER

(up to 5 minutes)

Bring kids together.

Say: **We've been discovering some of the parables Jesus told when he was here on earth. Today we'll explore a parable that tells about something "baaaad" that happens. Sorry, that was joke—because today's parable is about a lost sheep. Get it? Anyway, it's a great parable that helps explain a great truth about God:** **Jesus cares for each of us.**

Form a circle. **Shepherds are responsible for their sheep. They care for them and keep them safe. The Bible says that Jesus is our shepherd.** Ask: **• Why do sheep always seem to need a shepherd?**

• Why would people need a shepherd like Jesus?

Say: **Jesus loves us and cares for us, just as a shepherd cares for his sheep. Today, you'll have a chance to experience a little of what a shepherd does.**

But first, let's thank God for sending Jesus to be our shepherd.

Explain that kids will scatter around the room. Say that just as shepherds gather their sheep together, you'll gather kids together during the prayer. Begin the prayer by thanking God for Jesus, our good shepherd. Then go up to each child, lay your hand on his or her shoulder, and say: [child's name], **Jesus cares for you.** Then quietly guide the child to the center of the room. Continue until you've gathered everyone together. Close the prayer by asking God to help each person in the circle grow closer to Jesus.

(15 minutes)

Sheep and Shepherds

Kids will create "pens" to help them care for their egg-shaped "sheep."

Items to Pack:
1 plastic egg for each child, construction paper, scissors, tape, glue, markers, cardboard, cotton balls, staplers

Hold up an egg. **An egg is a fragile thing. And like a sheep, it requires careful handling. Today, you'll each get an egg-shaped "sheep" to care for. Throughout our entire time together today, you'll need to watch out for your sheep and keep it safe. You can name your sheep and decorate it so you can recognize it. You can each use these materials to create a "pen" to keep your sheep safe. But you'll only have a few minutes, so you'd better get started!**

Set out the cardboard, cotton balls, construction paper, glue, staplers, markers, and tape. Encourage kids to create small pens for their sheep. As kids are working, carefully give each person an egg to care for. When everyone has finished decorating their eggs and making their pens, gather them together in a circle with their sheep.

Say: **Be sure to take care of your sheep as we go through today's adventure. Keep it in sight and close to you the whole time, so it doesn't wander off. If it does, it'll be your responsibility to find it again. If you see someone else's sheep not being watched, you can quietly and carefully hide that sheep—as long as its shepherd doesn't notice.**

Ask: • **What might happen if you don't take your responsibilities seriously?**

• **How are you feeling about your new responsibilities of being a shepherd?**

Say: ● **God cares for each of us. God sent Jesus to be our good shepherd. Remember how I told you that Jesus told a parable about a**

SCENIC ROUTE For more impact and to help kids understand taking care of something fragile, use real eggs instead of plastic.

FUN FACT The first shepherd mentioned in the Bible was Abel, a son of Adam and Eve. In fact, lots of Bible heroes were shepherds, too: Abraham, Jacob, Moses, and David.

Items to Pack:
Bibles, about 15 small classroom objects, a piece of cloth to cover the objects, plastic "sheep" from previous activity, a few extra plastic eggs

TOUR GUIDE TIP Throughout the session, occasionally remind kids to keep an eye on their sheep. But if taking and hiding each others' sheep gets distracting, say it's time to let the sheep take a rest.

lost sheep? That parable will help us understand shepherds a lot more. Let's find out more!

STORY EXCURSION

(15 minutes)

Lost and Found

This experience will teach kids that God cares for each and every person, and will go to great lengths to save the lost sheep of his flock.

Open your Bible to Matthew 18:10-14, and show kids the passage.

Say: **Before we get started with today's parable in the Bible, let's try a quick experiment.**

Set out the 15 small objects, and give kids about one minute to study them. Then cover the objects with the cloth. Have kids turn their backs to you, and remove several of the objects and place them out of sight. Have kids turn around. Remove the cloth and give kids another minute to tell you which objects are missing. Repeat the process a few times, removing a different number of varying objects each time.

Ask: • **What surprised you about this experiment?**

Say: **It wasn't all that easy to realize which objects were missing, was it? Sometimes it's hard to pay close attention to the details around you. But that's *never* a problem for God. I'll show you what I mean.**

Form pairs, and give each pair a Bible. Have kids open their Bibles to Matthew 18:12-14. Say: **In today's parable, Jesus told about a lost sheep. In your pair, choose which of you will read verses 12 through 14 out loud.** Give partners a minute or so to read the passage in their pairs.

Say: **Hmm...a lost sheep.** Look around the room. **We seem to have a lot of sheep in the room. Maybe we can use them to act out this parable. Whoever in your pair is wearing the most green will go first.** Pause. **When I count to three, you'll gently take your partner's sheep and hide it somewhere in the room. Partners, you'll close your eyes—and no peeking! Ready? One, two, three!**

After kids wearing the most green have hidden the sheep, have them return and sit with their partners. Then have partners open their eyes and search for their sheep—but only for one minute! After a minute, have everyone sit again.

Then repeat the process, letting the other partners hide the sheep of those wearing the most green. Again, allow the "green" partners to search for their sheep for only one minute before returning to their pairs.

Gather partners back together. Some kids will probably still be missing their sheep.

Ask: • **What were you thinking as you searched for your sheep?**

• **If you found your sheep, what was that like?**

• **If you didn't find your sheep, what is that like?**

Say: **Look at the parable of the lost sheep in your Bible again.** Pause.

Ask: • **How did it feel to be responsible for your egg-shaped sheep, especially after you named them and built them a pen?**

• **How do you think Jesus feels when we—his sheep—wander away from him?**

• **Why do you think the shepherd in this parable left 99 sheep to look for one that was lost?**

• **What does this parable tell you about how Jesus feels about his sheep?**

Say: ◗ **God cares for each of us. He loves each of us. God sent Jesus to be our good shepherd—someone who would do anything to keep us safe and close to him. Let's explore that a little more. But first, let's find those lost sheep!**

Let kids find any remaining hidden sheep, allowing partners to give clues or actual whereabouts if necessary.

ADVENTURES IN GROWING

(10 minutes)
The Perfect Job

Kids will discover more about how much Jesus cares for them.

Form four groups, and give each group a Bible, paper, and pens or pencils.

Say: **I'm going to give each group a Scripture reference to look up. Your Scripture will have something to do with a shepherd or sheep. Have the person in your group whose birthday is closest to today read the Scripture out loud. Then, as a group, write a job description for a perfect shepherd, based on what you read and what we've already learned today.**

Assign each group one of the following Scripture references:

Items to Pack:
Bibles, paper, pencils or pens

- Psalm 23:1-2
- Psalm 23:3-4
- John 10:14-15
- Isaiah 40:11

Give groups several minutes to read the Scriptures and write their shepherd job descriptions. Then have each group read its Scripture and job description for everyone else. After all groups have presented, ask:

After hearing each group's presentation, what do you think are the top three requirements for being a good shepherd?

How do those traits relate to Jesus?

How can knowing that Jesus cares for you like a shepherd cares for his sheep help you this week?

Say: **This week, if you feel alone or scared—like a sheep that's wandered away from the flock—please remember Jesus. Remember how much he loves and cares for you!**

This next experience will help what we just learned stick in our brains.

SOUVENIRS

(10 minutes)

Never Alone

Kids will remember that Jesus cares for them as a good shepherd cares for his sheep.

Items to Pack:

Bibles, copies of the "Lost Sheep" handout (page 44), pens, colored markers, cotton balls, glue sticks

Set out pens or markers, plus cotton balls and glue sticks. Give each person a copy of the "Lost Sheep" handout on page 44.

Say: **Today we're learning that ◔ Jesus cares for each of us, just as a shepherd cares for his sheep. On your paper, you'll see a flock of sheep in a pasture. You can color the sheep, name them, or even glue wooly cotton balls on them—whatever you want to do.**

You'll also see a sheep that's wandered off by itself. That's you. On that sheep, write your name and a word or two that describes a situation where you're glad you have a good shepherd to find you and take you back to the flock. You might write "bullies at school" or "scared at night" on your sheep. You won't have to show your papers to anyone else.

When everyone has finished, say: **Put your Lost Sheep picture safely into your Travel Journal today as a reminder that ◔ Jesus cares for each of us, just like a good shepherd. If you feel lost this week, just** look at your paper and remember that you have a Shepherd who cares for you! Before we close, let's take a minute to thank God for caring enough to send a good shepherd like Jesus to care for us.

HOME AGAIN PRAYER

(10 minutes)

Use this experience to reinforce with kids how deeply God loves and cares for them.

Have kids write the words of Psalm 23:1 on their sheep pens: "The Lord is my shepherd; I have all that I need."

Then have everyone sit in a circle with their "sheep" nestled in their sheep pens.

Say: **Because we learned about lost sheep today, I want you to take your "found" sheep home with you. Use your sheep to tell at least one other person the parable of the lost sheep.**

We'll go around the circle. When it's your turn, place your sheep on the floor in front of you, and say the name of the person you'll tell about today's parable.

When you've gone around the circle, close with this prayer.

Pray: **God, thank you for sending Jesus, our Good Shepherd. Thank you for caring for each one of us. Please help us tell others about your love this week. And help us to remember all the ways you care for us. In Jesus' name, amen.**

Encourage kids to take their sheep and pens home. Say that every time they look at them, they can remember the parable of the lost sheep and how much Jesus cares for each of us.

Items to Pack:

Bibles, fine-tipped permanent markers, eggs kids decorated and sheep pens they made earlier

Lost Sheep

44

The Parable of the Vineyard Laborers

Pathway Point: God is fair and gracious to *everyone*.

> **Summary of Parable:** A vineyard owner pays all workers the same wages, regardless of the hours worked, incurring the resentment of those who worked the longest. (Matthew 20:1-15)

Travel Itinerary

Children (and adults, too) want life to be fair—and it seldom is. Jesus' parable about a landowner who gave the same wage to laborers who worked all day as he gave to those who worked just a few hours is a prime example of life being not fair...or is it?

The workers the landowner hired at the crack of dawn were promised a fair wage—and accepted the offer. The rest of the workers, hired throughout the day, trusted that the landowner would pay what was fair. This landowner—like God— had a reputation for being honest and fair.

And, like God, this landowner was both fair *and* generous.

As you lead your children in discovering more about the character of God today, be mindful that this lesson is for you, too. We sometimes forget just how loving God is toward us, showing undeserved grace and generosity.

Let God touch your heart through the activities and discussions in this lesson. And let God speak into your life through the kids you serve, too.

> **TOUR GUIDE TIP**
>
> The experiences in this book have been designed for multi-age groups. Select from the experiences, or adapt them as needed for your kids.

DEPARTURE PRAYER | (up to 5 minutes)
In this "fair prayer," children will discover that God treats them fairly... even if they don't always get what they ask for.

Items to Pack:
index cards, pencils or pens

Ask children to join you in sitting in a circle. Give each child an index card and pencil.

Say: **We're going to pray together, but we'll do it a little differently. Please write a one- or two-word prayer to God, listing something you'd like God to do for you or someone you know. For instance, I might write, "job" because a mom or a dad of a friend needs a job.**

Note: Share something real from your life or the life of a friend. You're modeling what you want kids to do.

You can draw what you want instead of writing it, too. It's up to you, but know this: Someone will be looking at what you write.

Allow several moments for children to write or draw.

Collect the cards.

Say: **You know, I'll bet God is busy running the universe. There's no sense bothering God with all these prayers. I'll just pick a couple; mine and another one or two.**

Pick several cards and toss the rest over your shoulder.

Now let's pray about these that I'm holding.

Pause.

Ask: • **Explain whether you think it was fair for me to do that.**

• **What would you think of God if God ignored your prayers so he could focus on other peoples' prayers?**

Pick up all the cards and have each child take one.

Say: **Let's silently pray about what's on the cards we're holding. You may not know who wrote yours, and that's okay...because God knows. I'll close for us.**

After 30 seconds, pray: **Dear God, thank you for always welcoming us when we have something to say to you, for listening to each and every one of us. Help us come to you often—and to listen to what you say, too. Please do what's best for the people whose cards we hold, always drawing them closer to you. In Jesus' name, amen.**

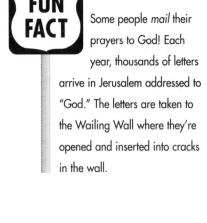

FUN FACT Some people *mail* their prayers to God! Each year, thousands of letters arrive in Jerusalem addressed to "God." The letters are taken to the Wailing Wall where they're opened and inserted into cracks in the wall.

1st STOP DISCOVERY

(15 minutes)

Fair Is Fair

Kids will discover that perhaps they don't want life to be fair after all.

Give kids each a "Fair Is Fair" tally sheet. Ask them to set the sheet on a table or on the floor in front of them.

Say: **Don't you wish that life was fair? If it was, then...wait a moment; I have to do some math.**

Make a show of pulling your wallet out of your pocket or purse and peering into it. Look as though you're counting money, and mutter to yourself as you do the math out loud.

Say: **Let's see...10, 20...and another 20...that's 40 plus two...four... five...plus—oh, there's a 50. Okay, then.**

Close your wallet.

Items to Pack:
1 "Fair Is Fair" tally sheet handout (page 54) per child, wallet

Ask: • **Don't you wish life was fair? That when you see someone else's huge flat screen or new bike or great grades that you could have those things, too?**

• I mean, look at me with all this money. If life were fair, you'd have the same amount of money, right? And all the same stuff as your friends?

Find a partner and talk about this...

Ask: • **If life were fair, what would you have that you don't have now?**

• If life were fair, what's something a friend gets to do that you'd be able to do, too?

Ask children to circle up and place their "Fair Is Fair" tally sheets directly in front of them. Place your sheet directly in front of you, too.

Say: **Welcome to the Fair Zone, where fair is fair. We're going to use our "Fair Is Fair" tally sheets to keep track of whether or not life is fair.**

Ask: • **Who here has the least amount of money? Check your pockets; I'm looking for someone who has no money—or close to it.**

When you establish the least amount someone has, ask all kids to place any money they have *above* that amount on their tally sheets.

Say: **After all, fair is fair. Nobody should have more money than the person with the least amount, right? That's fair.**

Ask if anyone has a cell phone with them. If even one person in the room doesn't have a cell phone, have those with cell phones place their phones on their sheets.

Ask if any children have televisions, game systems, or computers in their rooms. If they do and someone else doesn't, ask them to pretend to place those on their sheets.

Say: **Millions of people in the world live on less than two dollars per day. They don't get three meals every day. If you do, pretend to place your next meal on your handout.** Pause as kids do so.

They don't get their own rooms. If you have your own room, pretend to put it on your sheet. Pause as kids do so.

They don't have the chance to go to school or get an education. If you get to do that, please pretend to put it on your sheet. Pause as kids do so.

They don't always have shoes. If you have shoes, please take them

Items to Pack:

Bibles

FUN FACT

Tending a vineyard was hard work, often done in hot summer weather as the sun beat down. Workers planted and pruned vines as well as harvested grapes.

off and put them on your "Fair Is Fair" tally sheet. After all, fair is fair. Pause as kids place shoes on their sheets.

Do you get medical care? Do you go to the dentist? Not everyone does, so please pull out a tooth and place it on your sheet—wait! Don't do that!

Ask: • **What did you discover during this experience?**

• **Why do you think that when we compare what we have with what others have, we usually compare ourselves to those who have more?**

Say: **Life isn't fair in every way. Some people have more or less than others. Some people are better at math or juggling or sports than others.**

You're **better at some things than others, you know. God has given each of us unique gifts and skills. We aren't all the same, but we're all loved and invited into a forever friendship with God.**

Say: **Because God is loving, ◐God is fair and gracious to *everyone* in the way that matters most. We can all know and love him. We can all have life forever in heaven.**

> **STORY EXCURSION**
>
> (15 minutes)
>
> ## Show Me the Money!
>
> Kids will act out a story shared by Jesus that reveals a great deal about the character of God...and about our character, too.

Say: **Jesus told a story that will help us discover something about God. Because I know you're talented actors, let's take this one to the stage!**

Form six groups of children: The Landowner, 6:00 a.m. Workers, 9:00 a.m. Workers, Noon Workers, 3:00 p.m. Workers, and 5:00 p.m. Workers. If you have a small group, put just one or two children in each group of workers. Really small group? One child can represent *all* the groups of workers!

Ask the landowner to stand on one side of the room and have children stand on the other side of the room.

Say: **Those of you who are looking for work have come to the marketplace. You're day laborers—you don't have regular jobs. You come each day and hope someone will hire you for the day, so you can buy food for yourself and your families.**

And good news! That's about to happen...at least for *some* of you!

Read Matthew 20:1-15 aloud. Pause often to allow children time to act out what you're reading.

Be sure the workers are actually *working*—bending over as they pretend to dig in dirt, leaning over as they pluck grapes and prune vines. Their active involvement will help them feel the indignity the first-hired workers in Jesus' parable felt.

Applaud your actors' efforts when they've finished acting out the parable.

Ask children to form groups of four and read Matthew 20:1-15 together in their groups as a review of what they just experienced.

After they've had time to read, ask them to discuss these questions in their groups. After each question, invite groups to share their answers with the rest of the children.

Ask: • **Jesus said this story was like the kingdom of heaven. What point do you think Jesus was making about God's kingdom?**

• **What do you think: Was the landowner being fair? Why or why not?**

• **Tell about a time someone wasn't fair with you. What happened? How did you feel?** • **How would you describe the landowner? Why?**

• **How was the landowner like God? How were the workers like us?**

• **How does this story show that** God is fair and gracious to *everyone*?

Say: **When we work hard for something, it's easy to resent another person who gets the same thing without working as hard. You 9:00 a.m. workers put in a long day and you weren't happy that others who worked just one hour were paid the same as you.**

But the landowner was right: You got what you were promised. There was no law against the landowner being generous with others.

The landowner was fair...and generous. And so is God!

ADVENTURES IN GROWING

(10 minutes)

Food for Thought

Children will enjoy the "fruit of their vineyard labors" as they have grape jelly on a slice of healthy wheat or gluten-free bread.

Serve children bread with jelly along with cups of water—take it to them. Explain that, since they've worked hard in the vineyard all day

TOUR GUIDE TIP

Some children have food allergies that can be dangerous. Know your children, and consult with parents about allergies their children may have. Also, read food labels carefully, as hidden ingredients can cause allergy-related problems.

(or at least for one hour) you want to honor them by providing a vineyard-based snack: bread and grape jam!

As they enjoy their snack, ask them to talk as a large group.

Ask: • **Tell about a person who was generous with you. Who was it and what happened?**

When children finish their bread and jam, tell them you have another snack for them.

Give each child a small cluster of grapes. Tell children to pick out one grape and set it aside.

Say: **I hope you have lots of generous, fair people in your life. But no matter how many you have, you can have one more: Jesus.**

Let's explore that a bit with a game I call Grape Golf!

Hold up your "Fair Is Fair" tally sheet and indicate the small circle at the bottom of the page. Tell children to lay their sheets on a flat surface and place their remaining grapes in the circle.

Say: **You play Grape Golf by "flicking" your grape with a finger so it rolls toward your target—which is the "F" in the upper left-hand corner of your sheet. This is a par one course, which means you can only flick your grape once and, to win, your grape has to end up sitting perfectly centered in the middle of the target area.**

Hopefully you saved back a perfectly round grape! Give it a try.
Pause while children try.

Say: **Let's try again. By the way, did I mention that to win this game you must hit the target *every time*?**
Pause while children try again.

Say: **I'm thinking that maybe this is too hard. Let's change the rules. This time, you get as many tries as you need to hit the target. See how that works for you. Raise your hand when you've got your grape on the target.** Pause.

Say: **If you feel like eating your grape, do so now.**

The Bible says that, to earn God's approval, we have to be perfect all the time.

Ask: • **How many of you would say you've been perfect your entire lives?**

Ask: • **You've always done the right thing, said the right thing, thought the right thoughts, all the time—every time?**

I flunk that test.

My life is like playing Grape Golf. Even when I try to be perfect, I don't hit the target. I'm always missing the mark. And the Bible says you are, too; that everyone has sinned and been less than perfect, like God is perfect.

Read aloud Romans 3:23: **"For everyone has sinned; we all fall short of God's glorious standard."**

Find a partner and talk about this...

Ask: • **Tell about a time that you fell short, when you were less than perfect. What happened—and how did that feel?**

Say: **Here's some good news: no matter how many times you've fallen short, God is willing to forgive you. The Bible says if we ask for forgiveness, God will give it.**

Read aloud John 1:9: **"The one who is the true light, who gives light to everyone, was coming into the world."**

That's compassion! And that's fairness, too: God will give all of us the chance to be forgiven if we seek him and ask for forgiveness!

It's true:  **God is fair and gracious to *everyone!***

SOUVENIRS →

(10 minutes)

Taking Flight

This craft reminds children that even when life seems unfair, God really is fair.

Kids will still have their "Fair Is Fair" tally sheets, but if one or more children have bent, folded, or otherwise mutilated their sheets, have fresh pieces of paper on hand to give them.

Place a chair across the room from where the children are seated.

Say: **That may *look* like a chair, but it's really a runway for use by airplanes.**

Please craft your Tally Sheet into a paper airplane that's able to fly to that chair and land on the runway. You've got two minutes to make your plane. Go!

Urge kids to hurry—adding a bit of pressure adds to the fun.

At the end of two minutes, have children stand an equal distance from the chair and, one at a time, launch their airplanes.

Applaud all efforts. Ask children to retrieve their planes and then sit.

Items to Pack:
"Fair Is Fair" handouts from earlier activity, chair, sheets of paper

Ask: • **What was hard about this activity? What was easy?**

• **In what ways was this activity fair? Not fair?**

Say: **Sometimes when we say something isn't fair, we mean it isn't easy. It's hard to do.**

This was a very fair activity: You all had the same target and the same amount of time to make a plane. You all had to deal with gravity.

Ask: • **What are hard things God asks us to do?**

• **Which of those hard things is especially hard for you?**

Say: **Thank you for sharing what's hard for you. Sometimes, obeying God is hard for me, too. It's tough to be gracious and kind. It's hard to be forgiving. It's hard to be fair to others.**

I'm glad we serve God, and 🌍 **God is fair and gracious to** *everyone!*

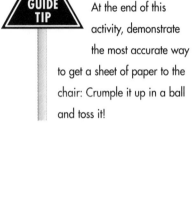

At the end of this activity, demonstrate the most accurate way to get a sheet of paper to the chair: Crumple it up in a ball and toss it!

HOME AGAIN PRAYER (up to 5 minutes)

Ask kids to smooth out their tally sheets.

Say: **We've used these sheets lots of ways today—and here's one more: Please exchange your sheet with a partner.**

After kids exchange sheets, continue.

Say: **Please write an encouraging note on your friend's sheet about one thing you think that person has to share with others. Maybe he's really funny. Or she's good at sports. Or you think the person has interesting things to say.**

Write that down. Or, if you'd prefer, draw a picture. I'll give you a minute.

Pause.

Now, please hold that person's tally sheet and silently pray for that person. I'll close for us.

After 30 seconds of silence, pray:

Dear God,

Thank you for loving us. Thank you for being generous and kind and fair with us...with everyone.

Help us be like you. Help us be fair. And kind. And generous.

Thank you for the person whose tally sheet we hold. You made that person and you did a great job!

In Jesus' name, amen.

Items to Pack:

"Fair Is Fair" handouts from earlier activity, pencils

Tell children to return the tally sheets to their partners and, if they'd like, to review what was written or drawn. Then have children place their handouts in their Travel Journals.

The Parable of the Mustard Seed

Pathway Point: God makes the smallest faith grow wildly.

Summary of Parable: "Here is another illustration Jesus used: 'The kingdom of heaven is like a mustard seed planted in a field. It is the smallest of all seeds, but it becomes the largest of garden plants; it grows into a tree, and birds come and make nests in its branches.' " (Matthew 13:31-32)

Travel Itinerary

The kids in your group may not think their faith can have much of an impact on the kingdom of God. In fact, they might not think they even have much faith at all. Kids often feel powerless, especially when it comes to "grown-up" concepts such as faith. But Jesus said we are to have the faith of a little child if we want to understand and enter God's kingdom.

Use today's adventure to encourage kids that Jesus values their faith, no matter how big or small. Help your children understand that God wants to grow their faith wildly, and that he'll use that faith to build and grow his kingdom. If a tiny mustard seed can grow into a tree that houses birds, just think what God can do with the faith in the hearts of you and your kids.

TOUR GUIDE TIP

The experiences in this book have been designed for multi-age groups. Select from the experiences, or adapt them as needed for your kids.

DEPARTURE PRAYER | (up to 5 minutes)

Kids will see how quickly they can make tall towers grow.

Bring kids together.

Say: **Lately, we've been looking at some of the parables Jesus told when he was here on earth. Today we'll explore a parable that helps us understand more about the kingdom of God. Today we'll explore how faith can help the kingdom of God grow. Before we get into the parable, though, let's see how quickly you can make tall towers grow.**

Form groups of three. Give groups equal amounts of supplies: paper, tape, and several blocks and books.

Say: **The goal is to see how tall your group can make a tower grow. The catch is you have to use some of each of the supplies I gave you—you can't just stack a bunch of books. Oh, and another catch—you'll only have one minute.**

Items to Pack:
blocks, books, paper, tape, watch or clock with a second hand

When everyone understands the directions, say "Go!" and start timing. After a minute, call time and compare towers. Then quickly play one or two more times. As kids learn to work together, their towers should grow taller in the allotted time. After a few rounds, have kids discuss these questions in their groups.

Ask: • **What did you think when I first explained this activity?**

• **How was building your first tower different from building your second or third?**

Say: **When I first explained the activity, you might have thought there was no way you could build a tall tower with the supplies and time I gave you. But you did it!**

It's kind of the same way with our faith in God. It can grow. In fact, today we'll discover that **God makes the smallest faith grow wildly. Let's ask God to help us learn more about growing faith.**

Pray: **Dear God, thank you for the parables that Jesus told. Help us to learn more about you, and have more faith in you. Please help our faith grow every day. In Jesus' name, amen.**

1st STOP DISCOVERY (15 minutes)

Growing, Growing, Grown!

This experience will teach kids that much can come of something that starts small—even faith!

Have kids form pairs, and give each pair a sheet of paper and a pencil. Have partners choose who will be the scribe in each pair.

Say: **Let's take a quick tour of our area to find examples of things that start really small, but grow into something bigger. As we walk, quietly talk with your partner about ideas you each have. When you agree on an idea, have your scribe write it on your paper. At the end of your tour, we'll compare lists. Ready? Let's look for growing things!**

Take kids on a tour of your church property—outside, if possible. If necessary, help kids get started on their lists by pointing out trees that grew from small acorns, or birds that were hatched from small eggs. But let kids do most of the discovering themselves!

After the tour, bring kids back together to sit on the floor in your area.

Say: **I'm looking forward to finding out what's on your papers. But first, I think we all need a little refreshment!** Pour a small handful of popcorn kernels into your hand, and hold out your hand for kids to see. **Hmmm. I don't think these few popcorn kernels will feed us all.**

Ask: • **What do you think about these kernels?**

Pause as kids call out answers. At least a few kids will probably tell you that the kernels will grow as they pop into actual popcorn.

Say: **Thanks for your popcorn know-how! These small kernels will grow as they pop into yummy popcorn. They look small, and like they would never be enough. But when they're cooked, small kernels make big bowls of popcorn!**

Bring out your bowl of popcorn, plus a napkin for each child. Give each child a scoop of popcorn.

Say: **Well, little popcorn kernels grew into a big treat for us. Let's see what other growing things you found on our tour.** Have the person who wasn't the scribe in each pair read his or her list aloud. Then thank everyone for participating.

Say: **Lots of little things grow into wonderful, big things. It's the same with our faith.**  **God makes the smallest faith grow wildly. Let's see what this parable that Jesus told says about growing faith.**

TOUR GUIDE TIP

If you can't go outside, simply take an inside tour of your church. There will probably be examples of things that are growing, such as plants, pictures of trees—and don't forget to look in at the nursery!

STORY EXCURSION

(15 minutes)

Faith Like a Mustard Seed

Kids will discover that God can help their faith grow.

Open your Bible to Matthew 13:31-32, and show kids the passage. Have kids stay in their pairs from the previous activity, and give each pair a Bible.

Say: **This parable that Jesus told is about a mustard seed, one of the smallest of seeds.** Bring out your container of mustard seeds, and pour a few into your hand. Have kids pass the seeds around the circle so everyone can hold them and see how small they are.

Say: **These mustard seeds are tiny, aren't they? Let's see what this parable says about them. And guess what: This parable is *really* small—just two verses! But it can help our faith grow bigger and bigger!**

In their pairs, have each partner read aloud one of the verses in the passage.

Ask: • **What surprised you about this parable?**

• **What do you think the mustard seed represents?**

Say: **When we believe in Jesus, we're a part of the kingdom of heaven. And our faith, even if it's the size of a little mustard seed, can**

SCENIC ROUTE →

For extra fun, bring in an air corn popper, and let kids help make the popcorn. Just supervise and be careful—the popper gets hot!

Items to Pack:
Bibles, container of mustard seeds (with the spices at the grocery store), brown paper or grocery bags, scissors, transparent tape, colored construction paper, green construction paper, markers

help the kingdom grow—just like a mustard seed can grow into a tree! Let's make something to help us wrap our brains around this idea.

Choose one child to tape a mustard seed to the wall, near the floor. **Okay, there's our little mustard seed. Now it's time to watch it grow!**

Have kids work together to create a tree growing on the wall from the little mustard seed. Twist brown paper bags and tape them to the wall above the mustard seed as the trunk of the tree. Cut strips of brown paper, and twist them into branches. Cut green construction paper leaves and add them to the branches. Crumple paper into nest shapes, and add them to a few of the branches. And don't forget to add some construction paper birds!

As the mustard tree "grows," comment on how big it's growing. When kids can't reach any higher on the wall, call time and gather everyone on the floor in front of the tree.

Say: **Wow! That's an amazing mustard tree! And it's amazing because it grew from that one tiny little mustard seed!**

Ask: **What do you think of our tree?**

How is your faith like that mustard seed?

How can your faith help the Kingdom of God grow, just as our tree grew?

Say: **God can use our faith, no matter how big or small, to help his kingdom grow. He can turn our faith into something wonderful like this mustard tree. 🌑 God makes the smallest faith grow wildly. He can use our faith to help others believe in God, and to offer comfort to others, just as a tree offers comfort and safety for birds. Let's talk about that a little more.**

Items to Pack:

green construction paper, scissors, tape, markers

TOUR GUIDE TIP

If you have a large group of kids, form groups and assign each group a role. One can be the Trunk Twisters, another can be the Trunk Tapers, another can be the Leaf Lifters, and so on. Otherwise, just let kids work on whatever part of the tree they choose.

ADVENTURES IN GROWING

(10 minutes)

Leaves of Faith

Kids will discover more about how their faith can help the kingdom of God grow.

Say: **🌑 God makes the smallest faith grow wildly. Even if we think we don't have a lot of faith to share, God can use us for his kingdom. But before we can share our faith with others, we need to figure out what we know. Let's think about the things we know about God and Jesus—the things we can tell others. We'll add those ideas to our tree. I think you'll be surprised at how much faith you have to share!**

Have kids cut out more paper leaves. On each leaf, have them write a word or short phrase that describes something they know about God or Jesus. Kids might write "God loves us," "Jesus forgives our sins," or "God made the world." Have kids keep writing and adding leaves. Then have everyone stand back and admire the tree.

Say: **Look at how your faith helped that tree grow bigger and fuller! You know, it's the same way with the kingdom of God. Every little bit of your faith can help the kingdom grow. Every thing you tell another person about God or Jesus can help the kingdom grow. No matter how young you are or how small you feel, you can be a big part of God's kingdom!**  **God makes the smallest faith grow wildly. Let's make sure we remember that!**

Items to Pack:

a photocopy of the "Growing Faith" handout on page 61 for each student and yourself, glue dots, colored markers, green construction paper, scissors

---

SOUVENIRS →

(10 minutes)

Growing Faith

Use this experience to reinforce with kids how God wants to help their faith grow.

Set out glue dots, scissors, green construction paper, and colored markers. Give each person a copy of the "Growing Faith" handout, and keep a copy of your own.

Say: **Today we're learning that**  **God makes the smallest faith grow wildly. This handout can help us remember that our faith can help the kingdom of God grow!**

First, have kids draw and color in branches and leaves near the top of their papers, in line with the roots at the bottom of the paper.

Then have each person cut a 2x11-inch strip of green construction paper. Cut a strip for yourself, too. Demonstrate how to fold the strip accordion-style, starting at one end of the long strip. Each fold should be about an inch deep. Use glue dots to glue the back of the first fold right above the roots on your paper. Use another glue dot to glue the back of the last fold to the paper, keeping all the folds "scrunched" together. Help kids as needed.

Say:  **God makes the smallest faith grow wildly. This picture can remind you to keep your faith growing! Each time you do something to help your faith grow, you're helping the kingdom of God grow. This week, when you do something to help your faith grow—like reading your Bible or praying—write what you did on one of the** green folds. Then loosen the top glue dot and move it up an inch. **Keep writing and moving the folds until your tree has grown straight and tall!**

Demonstrate with your own paper. When everyone understands, say: **Put your "Growing Faith" tree in your Travel Journal today as a reminder that God can use your faith to help his kingdom grow.**

Before we end today, let's take a minute to thank God for helping our faith grow.

Items to Pack:

mustard seeds, transparent tape

HOME AGAIN PRAYER

(10 minutes)

Sit with kids in a circle on the floor.

Say: **I'm so thankful that God wants to help our faith grow. Even faith as small as a mustard seed can grow into something big and beautiful. I want to give each of you a mustard seed to take home as a reminder that your faith can grow bigger and bigger.**

Go to each child in turn. Let the child tear a piece of transparent tape and hold it out, sticky side up. Place a mustard seed in the center of the tape strip as you say, [Child's name], **God wants to help your faith grow wildly.** Tear another strip of tape and place it over the first to seal the mustard seed in place. When everyone has a sealed seed, close the prayer.

Pray: **God, thank you for helping our faith grow. Thank you for using our little faith to help your kingdom grow. We love you.**

In Jesus' name, amen.

Encourage kids to take their mustard seeds home with them, and put them where they'll see them often, such as by their beds or taped to a bathroom mirror. Every time they look at the seed, they can remember that ◗ God makes the smallest faith grow wildly.

Growing Faith

The Parable of the Unmerciful Servant

Pathway Point: God wants us to show mercy to others.

Summary of Parable: Jesus tells about a king who forgives an enormous, millions-of-dollars debt of a servant. That servant then goes to another servant and demands payment of a debt of a few thousand dollars. Unable to pay the debt, the second servant pleads for mercy. The first servant has the second servant thrown into jail. When the king hears about what's happened, he orders the first servant to be jailed and tortured until he has paid his entire debt. (Matthew 18:21-35)

Travel Itinerary

When Peter asked how often he was required to forgive someone, Jesus answered with a story—a story that revealed a great deal about God.

A king in Jesus' story forgives a servant, freeing him from a staggering debt. Yet that same servant has a fellow servant tossed in debtor's prison for not repaying a much smaller debt.

When the king hears about the first servant's behavior, he responds with anger. Mercy is withdrawn—and justice done.

It seems that while God is merciful to us, that mercy comes with the expectation we'll pass it along. Those of us who have been forgiven need to be equally forgiving of others.

As you present this lesson to your children, you're helping them discover something about God. Yes, God is merciful and kind. God gives us favor we don't deserve and can't pay for in any way, shape, or form.

But that's not the *only* message in Jesus' parable for Peter...and your kids... and you.

God expects us to be merciful, too.

What we've received, we're to share with others.

As you present this lesson and see your kids discover the truth in it, be open to God speaking into your heart, too.

TOUR GUIDE TIP

The experiences in this book have been designed for multi-age groups. Select from the experiences, or adapt them as needed for your kids.

DEPARTURE PRAYER	(5 minutes)

In this "mercy prayer," children will come to appreciate that God is merciful to them—always. And they can have the same sort of mercy for others!.

Items to Pack:

Bible, 1 penny per child

Give each child a penny.

Ask children to examine their pennies and find where the penny says, "In God We Trust."

Say: **Today we're talking about mercy.**

Ask: • **Who knows what *mercy* means?**

Allow several children to suggest their definitions, and encourage them for answering.

Say: **Thank you! I think of mercy as kindness I don't deserve. It's when someone does something for me that...well, I don't deserve.**

God shows us all that sort of kindness. We don't deserve it, but there it is—a gift from God day after day. We can count on it, like our pennies say. We can trust in God because God doesn't change.

The Bible says this about God and God's Son, Jesus...

Read aloud, from a Bible, Hebrews 13:8: **"Jesus Christ is the same yesterday, today, and forever."**

That means God is always kind, always full of mercy...which isn't true of me. Some days I wake up feeling great and it's easy for me to be patient and kind.

But other days...well, let's just say I'm not the same yesterday, today, and tomorrow.

Ask: • **How about you? Are you kind sometimes...all the time...or somewhere in between? Why?**

After children answer, continue.

Thanks for sharing. Let's see what it might be like if God wasn't always full of mercy. Please get your coin ready to flip into the air. If you don't know how to flip a coin, that's okay—you can just toss it and then catch it.

But if someone here is a really great coin flipper, would you show us the way to do it? Pause for a volunteer.

Thank you.

Now, get ready to flip your penny—but no flipping yet!

Let's say you did something wrong and you came to God to ask for forgiveness. And let's say God was like some of us: kind, but only

TOUR GUIDE TIP This activity assumes you're giving children an American penny. If you're using another country's coins, instruct children which side of the coin represents "mercy" and which represents "no mercy."

TOUR GUIDE TIP Don't worry—in any gathering of two or more children, one of them always believes himself or herself a good coin flipper. Allow time for a 30-second demonstration and coaching session.

about half the time. In a moment I'll ask you to flip your penny. If it lands with the "In God We Trust" facing up, let's say God forgives you. But if it lands the other way—no forgiveness for you.

Flip your pennies and let's see what happens.

After kids flip their pennies, have those whose coins landed tails-up put their pennies aside.

Say: **Oh, oh...looks like some of you are in trouble.**

Now let's say that those of you who were forgiven did something else wrong—and I'll bet we all do, say, or think something that displeases God every day.

Time to flip your pennies again, those of you who are still holding them.

After children flip, again have those whose coins came up "tails" set their coins aside.

Play four or five rounds—until every child is out of the game.

Say: **I'm glad God is the same every day, and that God is always merciful! Aren't you?**

Ask children to gather with you in a circle.

Say: **Please pick up your pennies and hold them in the palm of one hand so the words "In God We Trust" are facing up.**

Now, let's pray, thanking God for being kind to us, even when we don't deserve it. Even when we haven't earned it. If you would, please offer a silent prayer.

I'll close for us.

Allow children time to pray, and then close as follows:

Thank you, God, for your mercy. For always loving us. For always being kind to us, even when we don't deserve it.

Please help us to treat others the way you treat us.

In Jesus' name, amen.

Say: **Thanks for praying with me.**

There's something about God's mercy you should know: In the same way God is merciful to us,  God wants us to show mercy to others.

Let's talk about that some more. You'll need that penny, so I hope you haven't spent it!

FUN FACT Since its beginning, the U.S. Mint has produced over 288.7 *billion* pennies. Lined up edge to edge, these pennies would circle the earth roughly 137 times.

(15 minutes)

Penny Pincher

Kids will discover that it's easy to get in money trouble...and harder to show mercy.

Items to Pack:
4 additional pennies per child (and 5 pennies for you, too!)

Make sure each child still has a penny.

Say: **Let's play a game I call Penny Pincher!**

You start by first holding one arm so it's parallel with the floor, your elbow up, and your hand on that arm palm-up, your fingers in a cup. I'll show you...

You'll want to practice this several times before showing the children. If you simply can't get the hang of the game, work with someone else who can demonstrate it for you.

Place your penny on your upturned elbow and balance it there.

The object of the game is to catch the penny in your cupped hand before the penny hits the floor. You do that by quickly dropping your arm and "pinching" the penny in your cupped hand.

Give it a try!

Children will need several tries before they've got the hang of this game. Expect pennies to be hitting the floor and kids scrambling after the pennies.

After giving children at least three tries with their pennies, ask them to pause and sit on the floor.

Ask: • **What makes this game hard? easy?**

• **If you could change one thing about this game to make it easier, what would it be?**

Say: **I'm not going to have mercy on you by making the changes you suggested. Instead, I've got an even *bigger* challenge for you: Try catching two pennies.**

Distribute another penny to each child.

Say: **This time, stack two pennies on your elbow.**

Try three more times to see if you can catch the pennies. See how many you can snatch before they hit the floor.

After kids have made their attempts, continue.

Give kids each three more pennies so they have a stack of five to use. Allow them to have several tries to pinch all those pennies.

Say: **Great job! Please put all your pennies in your pocket for now.**

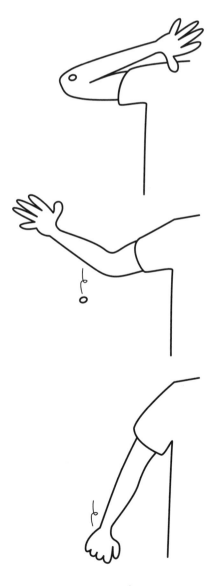

TOUR GUIDE TIP

If you have young children or children who can't quite master the arm-drop-penny-snatch, suggest they simply toss the two pennies in the air and try to catch them both with one hand.

After kids comply, have them sit and discuss the following:

Ask: • **Many of us ran into trouble when we got more money. How is that like or unlike what happens when we get more money in real life?**

• **How could I have had mercy on you in this game?**

• **Tell about a time someone in your life showed you mercy—kindness you didn't deserve. Who was it—and what happened?**

Say: **Jesus told a story about a man who got in trouble with money. He went into debt, and then he couldn't pay it back.**

Let's see how someone was merciful to him...or wasn't. And let's discover how **God wants us to show mercy to others.**

STORY EXCURSION

(15 minutes)

Good News and Bad News

Kids will act out a story shared by Jesus that demonstrates God is merciful to us and wants us to show mercy to others.

Say: **I've got some good news and some bad news for you.**

The good news: As a special surprise, I've arranged for you to all be movie stars in a film that will be shot today.

The bad news: The film crew hasn't shown up.

The good news: You'll wear cool costumes in this movie.

The bad news: The costumer didn't show up.

But the good news is you'll use really amazing Hollywood props.

And the bad news is that the props didn't show up, either.

Good news: You'll have lots of time to learn your lines and rehearse.

But...the bad news is that I forgot to send you your scripts.

So you pretty much have to do this movie without a film crew... or costumes...or props...or a script.

Oh, and more bad news: The other actors didn't show up, either. You each have to act out this entire movie on your own. But the show must go on!

Everyone, take one penny out of your pocket. That's your prop.
Pause.

There are three characters in this movie. You'll use your penny to show which character you're playing at the moment. The king wears

Items to Pack:
Bible, 1 penny per child

a crown, so while you're the king put your penny on your head like this.

Demonstrate and encourage kids to do as you do.

Say: **The million-dollar servant has so much money he doesn't care if he loses some. So when you're playing the million-dollar servant, keep tossing your penny in the air and catching it.**

Demonstrate and encourage kids to do as you do.

The thousand-dollar servant has very little money and he keeps careful track of every penny. When you're playing the thousand-dollar servant, stick your penny on your nose so you can keep an eye on it.

Demonstrate and encourage kids to do as you do.

By the way, that's *on* your nose...not *in* your nose!

Ready? I'll read the script and you each act it out, doing what the character I'm reading about does.

And remember to stay in costume. When you're the king, your penny is on your head. When you're the million-dollar servant, you're tossing it and catching it. When you're the thousand-dollar servant, it's on your nose.

Read aloud Matthew 18:21-35, pausing as you go to let kids get and stay in costume. Have fun with this and your kids will, too.

Lead kids in applauding their performances and in taking bows when they've finished. Ask them to put their pennies back in their pockets.

Ask: • **Which character in our movie reminds you most of you? Why?**

• **What do you think of the king's actions? Was he merciful or unmerciful...or both?**

• **What do you think Jesus was trying to tell his audience—and us—about God? about how we're to treat others?**

Say: **Thanks for sharing your thoughts.**

Sometimes we think that God has to be kind, but we don't have to be kind. We believe God has to treat us with mercy, but we don't have to treat others with the same sort of mercy.

That's not what Jesus was saying here, is it? 🌓 **God wants us to show mercy to others, just like he's shown mercy to us.**

TOUR GUIDE TIP

By demonstrating rather than just telling, you signal that you're enthused and that the activity will be fun. Plus you remove the possible embarrassment of a child not quite knowing what to do. Be playful. Have fun!

ADVENTURES
IN
GROWING

(10 minutes)
Food for Thought

Children will experience a practical way to show mercy to others as they enjoy a muffin or other easily-divided snack.

Items to Pack:

small cups of water, napkins, plastic knives, plates, an easily-divided snack such as a muffin or doughnut—1 per pair of children

Ask children to form pairs. If you have an odd number of children, become part of a pair yourself—it's important that there be pairs.

Say: **In a moment I'll have a snack for you. Before I do, please decide in your pair who you think looks most like me. You've got 20 seconds to decide.**

Feign playful indignity if kids laugh.

Once your look-alikes have been established in each pair, ask those lucky people—of course they're lucky; they look like you!—to come and pick up two cups of water, one for themselves and one for their partner.

Then have them come and pick up one snack on a plate, one knife, and two napkins. Warn them to not touch their snack until you tell them to do so.

Ask: • **Hmmm...one snack and two people. What would be the fair way to divide that snack between you and your partner? Talk about that with your partner.**

• **Another question: What would be the merciful way to divide the snack? What would show undeserved kindness?**

Say: **Showing mercy to someone isn't about being fair. It's not fair that Jesus died for our sins—but it's merciful.**

However, when it comes to snacks, fair counts a *lot*. Let's do this: the person in your pair who looks most like me will use the knife to divide the snack. Then the other person in your pair will choose which piece to eat.

You can be fair...you can be merciful...it's up to you. But remember: ◐ **God wants us to show mercy to others.**

As children enjoy their snacks, ask them to discuss the following with their partners:

Ask: • **Tell about a time you didn't feel like being merciful. What happened?**

• **Is it ever okay to not show mercy to someone? If so, what's a situation where that might be true?**

• **The Bible tells us that God loves us, yet God doesn't stop some people from getting sick or hurt. How is that merciful—or isn't it?**

TOUR
GUIDE
TIP

Some children have food allergies that can be dangerous. Know your children, and consult with parents about allergies their children may have. Also, read food labels carefully, as hidden ingredients can cause allergy-related problems.

Say: **God wants us to be kind to others—even when they don't de-serve it. That's hard to do, and I can think of times I wouldn't want to be kind. If someone is hurting me or people I love, it would be hard to be kind to that person.**

Yet, my actions have hurt others.

My words have hurt others.

My words and actions have even hurt God—I've disappointed him because I've sinned.

Yet God is willing to forgive me.

Is being merciful hard? Yes. But God isn't asking me to do some-thing that he doesn't do himself.

🜨 **God wants us to show mercy to others, and shows us how to do it by how he shows mercy to us.**

SOUVENIRS →

(10 minutes)

Mercy Looks Like This

This activity reminds children that God expects them to show mercy to others.

Distribute a "This Week...Mercy Looks Like This" handout to each child.

Say: **Showing mercy to others is a decision. It's a choice. We can of-fer undeserved kindness when the chance to do so comes up.**

At school, you may notice that a kid you don't even know needs help—and you can decide to jump in and help. Or, if you're home, you may see that your mom or dad is really tired. So you can do extra chores you weren't even asked to do.

You can choose to be kind...and you can choose to be merciful.

Ask: • **Tell about a time you showed someone undeserved kindness. Who did you help? What did you do?**

• **How has God showed undeserved kindness to you in the past week?**

Say: **Thanks for sharing your experiences. I love hearing how God is working in your lives!**

Sometimes we know people who could use some kindness in their lives. Maybe they're having a hard time. Maybe they're sad or afraid.

Let's each think of someone who needs some kindness.

Pause.

Items to Pack:
a copy of the "This Week... Mercy Looks Like This" handout from page 72 for each child, pens or markers

Ask: • **Got that person in mind? How will you show mercy to that person this week? What will you say or do to share undeserved kindness?**

Say: **Draw a picture of what you'd like to do to show mercy to that person. Or, if it's something you'd like to say, write the words you'd like to share.**

And don't worry if art isn't your top subject in school—just do your best! You've got three minutes to draw or write.

Pause for up to three minutes.

Say: **Thanks. Find a partner and show your partner your drawing. And explain what you intend to do to show mercy in the coming week—if God gives you the chance.**

Allow time for children to pair up and talk.

Say: **Thank you for sharing with your partner.**

God may not give you the chance to be merciful in the way you've planned—and that's okay. Because God *will* give you the chance to be merciful to *someone* in the coming week!

The question is this: Will you show others the same kind of mercy God has shown you? I hope so, because ◓ God wants us to show mercy to others.

Then have children place their handouts in their Travel Journals.

HOME AGAIN PRAYER

(up to 5 minutes)

Say: **Let's ask God for help in showing mercy when the chance comes this week.**

Ask children to stand and place their hands in front of them, palms up, fingers cupped as if they're about to receive something.

Say: **We can't give others what we don't have ourselves. Before we can show God's mercy to others, we have to receive it.**

Let's silently close our eyes and keep our hands cupped. Let's ask God to fill us with his love. I'll close.

Pause 30 seconds and then pray.

Pray: **God,**

Thank you for your love. Your love is so powerful, so kind, so merciful—and we don't deserve it. We haven't earned it.

It's a gift—one we receive from you.

Help us be as kind to others as you've been to us.

Even if those other people don't deserve it.
In Jesus' name, amen.

Ask children to go around the room giving each other—and you—high fives. They're going to have an exciting week as God works in their lives!

Say: **I want to remind you to look for chances to be merciful—both in ways you've planned and in ways that you can't know are coming. Decide now that you'll treat others the way God has treated you: with undeserved kindness.**

God bless you as you obey him and live out his love. ◐ **God wants us to show mercy to others!**

Give each other another round of high fives! It's going to be a great week!

This week...

Mercy looks like this

JOURNEY 8

The Parable of the Rich Farmer

Pathway Point:  God wants us to live for what matters most.

> **Summary of Parable:** A hard-working and responsible farmer amasses wealth. He prospers so much that he needs to build bigger barns to store it all. Finally, with all of his wealth managed well, he prepares to relax and enjoy a comfortable retirement, to "Take it easy! Eat, drink, and be merry!" But he dies before being able to enjoy his massive wealth. (Luke 12:13-21)

Travel Itinerary

Kids are always comparing their own "stuff" to that of their friends and peers. It's easy for them to focus on having the next, coolest, trendiest new thing...rather than spending their time, effort, and money pursuing what lasts.

Use this lesson to help kids realize that things they may acquire here on earth don't last, but a relationship with God is eternal! Guide kids in prioritizing things in their lives so they can develop a rich relationship with God.

TOUR GUIDE TIP

The experiences in this book have been designed for multi-age groups. Select from the experiences, or adapt them as needed for your kids.

DEPARTURE PRAYER (up to 5 minutes)

Have kids form pairs or trios. Give each group a cup filled with candy, but instruct kids *not* to eat the treats just yet. Then say: **This cup is filled with good stuff! Our lives are filled with good stuff, too! In your group, take turns taking a piece of candy out of the cup and putting it into your left hand. As you do, name something that's a blessing in your life. Keep going until your left hand is full.**

Give kids about three minutes to share and add candies. Then draw attention back to yourself.

Ask: • **How does it feel to look at all the great stuff God has blessed you with?**

Say: **Our lives overflow with good things from God. Let's take time to thank God for being so good to us!**

While kids hold their handfuls of candy, let them pray and thank God for all the good things he's given them. As kids enjoy their treats, say: **Today we'll explore how**  **God wants us to live for what matters most. God has**

Items to Pack:
small candies such as M&M's candies or jellybeans, cups (1 for every two or three kids)

given us so many good things...but which ones are most important? That's what we'll discover today!

(10 minutes)

Spy Race

Kids will race around the room, looking for certain items...if they can avoid all the temptations and distractions!

Say: **On the count of three, call out three things you like to do each week.** Allow a few seconds for kids to think. **One, two, three!** Pause while kids shout. **Wow! You stay busy with fun things like...**[repeat any of the things you were able to pick out of the shouting].

Our days *are* busy, and sometimes it can be hard to find time for the things that really matter. But  God wants us to live for what matters most. Let's try an experiment. Form groups of about eight kids and hand each group a list of items. Then say: **You have five minutes to find everything on your list. Ready, go!**

After five minutes, call time.

Ask: • **How did you do?**

• **What made it hard to find the stuff on your list?**

• **What other things in our room looked more interesting that what was on your list?**

Say: **Sometimes we fill our lives with lots of fun, cool, interesting things—but those things can keep us away from what's really important.  God wants us to live for what matters most. Let's dig into a story that Jesus told about someone who had a problem like that.**

STORY EXCURSION

(20 minutes)

The Parable of the Rich Farmer

Kids will act out a parable as they explore what it means to live for what matters most.

Open your Bible to Luke 12:13 and show kids the passage. Say: **Luke 12:13 tells about a time when Jesus was teaching. Thousands of people gathered around to hear what Jesus said, when all of a sudden, a man called out to Jesus from the crowd. He kind of tattled on his brother, asking Jesus, "Teacher, tell my brother to divide our father's estate with me." It seems that this man's father had died and left every-**

Items to Pack:

Hide the following items in your room: a black crayon, a cotton ball, a piece of gum, a rubber band, a safety pin, 3 puzzle pieces, and a piece of blue yarn. List these items on a card. Also hide kid-pleasing items such as candy, a video game, a movie, cool toys or stuffed animals, or sports equipment. Bring in things that kids aren't used to seeing in your room that might be a distraction for them.

TOUR GUIDE TIP

You can have kids search for any 8 to 10 items you choose. So check out your children's ministry supply closet to see if there are other items you can use.

Items to Pack:

Bible, a piece of newsprint or a whiteboard, markers

thing to one son and not the other.

Ask: • **How do you feel when someone gets more than you?**

Say: **Jesus told the crowd "Beware! Guard against every kind of greed. Life is not measured by how much you own." Then he told a story to show what he meant. I need your help to explore that story.**

Choose four kids to be the barn in the story. They can stand in a circle, with their arms outstretched.

Choose another child to be the man in the story.

Direct the rest of the kids to be the man's crops. They can crouch down like wheat kernels getting ready to grow.

Explain that you'll tell the story and kids can act it out. Encourage kids to use their creativity and ham it up!

Say: **A rich man had an awesome farm that was growing out of sight! His crops were incredible! In fact, they grew so well that the man wasn't going to have enough room in his barn for them all.** Direct the "man" to move the "crops" into the "barn."

The man said, "I know! I'll tear down my barns and build bigger ones. Then I'll have enough room for my crops and all my other stuff." Guide the man in "tearing down" the barn.

"Then I don't have to do anything for years and years! No work! I can sit back...relax...eat, drink, and just have fun!" Direct the man to smile and walk around, looking very pleased with himself.

"But God thought that was a bad idea. God said, 'You fool! You will die this very night.'" Let the man act as if he died.

Ask: • **Now who will get all of your stuff?**

Say: **Jesus ended his story by saying, "It's foolish to store up things on earth but not have a good relationship with God."**

Clap for all of your actors, and then let kids sit down. Hang a sheet of newsprint on a wall. Draw a vertical line down the middle of the paper.

Ask: • **What do you think mattered most to the man in Jesus' story? How can you tell?**

Say: **Imagine this story were happening today. Come up and write or draw on the left side of this paper something that matters most to people today. Think of yourself, your friends, and your family.**

Ask: • **What matters the most to them and you?**

Set out markers and let everyone come forward to write or draw.

While kids are finished drawing, ask: • **What do you think matters most to God? What makes you think that?**

FUN FACT

Although it may seem silly to us that a man "tattled" on his brother to Jesus, in ancient times it *was* common for people to bring financial disagreements before a rabbi.

Let kids come up and write or draw their responses on the right side of the paper. Point to the paper and ask: • **How are these lists different?**

• **Why do you think they're different?**

Say: **Jesus told parables—special stories—to teach about God. Through this story, we can tell that** 🌑 **God wants us to live for what matters most. If you think things like** [name some of the things kids wrote or drew] **are important to God, let's change this parable to see what the man *should* have done. As you're acting the story out, I'll pause and let you call out what you think he *should* do.**

Have kids assume their roles from the earlier drama, and begin your "new parable."

Say: **A rich man had an awesome farm that was growing out of sight! His crops were incredible! In fact, they grew so well that the man wasn't going to have enough room in his barn for them all.** Direct the "man" to move the "crops" into the "barn."

Then the farmer thought to himself...

Guide kids in calling out answers such as, "I can give the food away," or "Maybe I should make a huge feast for the whole town." Let kids have fun acting out any of the suggested responses. Then ask kids sit down.

ADVENTURES IN GROWING

(10 minutes)

It Fits!

This eye-opening object lesson helps kids discover that they really can put God first...and still have time for their other interests.

Gather kids in a circle and set the jar, rocks, gravel, sand, and pitcher of water in the middle of the circle.

Say: **Think quietly about this question.**

Ask: • **What do you think your friends would say is most important to you? Why?** Allow kids time to think.

Say: 🌑 **God wants us to live for what matters most. God wants us to fill our lives with things that please him, that show his love, and that help others know him more. Of course you can do other things, too! But things that are important to God should be first in our lives. Let me show you what I mean.**

Motion to the items set in the middle of the circle.

Let's say all this stuff represents things you like and do. The jar represents the time you have in one day. Let each person say something he or she does during their week, such as playing soccer, hanging out with friends, or taking music lessons. Each time kids share, let them put in a handful of gravel. When the gravel is gone, kids can add rocks. Then ask:

• **Do you think all this sand and water will fit, too? Why or why not?**

Say: **God wants us to live for what matters most. That means we put the big stuff first in life—the stuff that matters to God.** Take the items out of the jar. Let a few kids share things from the list made during the Story Excursion. As kids share things that matter to God, they each can add one of the large rocks.

Say: **I think there's still room in here.**

Ask: • **What were those other things that mattered to you?** Let kids share the other things they love, such as sports or hobbies. As kids share, they can add gravel. When the gravel is gone, kids can keep sharing and add sand.

Look at the jar and say: **Wow! You know, I still think there's room in here!** Pour the pitcher of water into the jar. **See, there's still time for things like eating ice cream, playing video games, reading books, and walking your dog!**

Ask: • **What made a difference in this experiment?**

Say: **Jesus' parable taught us not to worry about collecting things or being rich.** **God wants us to live for what matters most. When you put the big stuff first in life, you'll be surprised that you still have time for other things you love, too.**

It's important to try this ahead of time so you select the right number of rocks and the right amount of gravel, sand, and water. Testing ahead of time will make the experiment even more powerful, memorable, and applicable for kids.

SOUVENIRS →

(10 minutes)

Fill the Barn

Guide kids in looking around their world for examples of things that really matter to God.

Say: **In Jesus' parable, the man wanted bigger barns so he could fill them with food and things. But** God wants us to live for what matters most. Hold up the "Big Barn" handout. **Let's fill your barn with things that matter to God!**

Let kids skim through magazines to find pictures or words that represent things that matter to God. Kids might find families, smiles, and words like *help* or *serve*. Kids can cut out the words or pictures and glue them inside the barn. As kids finish, have them place their completed "Big Barn" artwork in their Travel Journals.

Items to Pack:
1 photocopy of the "Big Barn" handout on page 79 for each child, old magazines, glue, scissors

(10 minutes)

Use this experience to let kids consider the many blessings that God has poured into their lives.

Say: **We started today by thanking God for all the things—the blessings—he's filled our lives with. Hold out your hands as if you're going to receive another treat.** Pause.

As I pray, imagine God pouring out new blessings into your hands. Imagine that they're the things that matter to God...things like his love, forgiveness, and joy. Or things like serving others or putting others first. Pause.

Keep your hands held out as I pray.

Pray: **Loving God, thank you for every good and perfect gift you give to us. Pour out new blessings into our lives, and let us in turn live in a way that pleases you. In Jesus' name, amen.**

Big Barn

"Yes, a person is a fool to store up earthly wealth but not have a rich relationship with God." (Luke 12:21)

JOURNEY 9

The Parable of the Sower

Pathway Point: God wants to grow the seeds of faith planted in us.

> **Summary of Parable:** A farmer throws seed into different sorts of soil. The seeds fare differently, depending on the soil. (Mark 4:1-20)

Travel Itinerary

Jesus sure knew what he was doing when he used parables to teach about God. All of us, including the kids in your group, are familiar with growing plants. We've all seen plants and trees and fields of crops—or at least pictures of them! So we can all relate to seeds growing in soil. This parable gives us a simple, yet powerful, image of what kind of spiritual soil we need in our lives to allow seeds of faith to grow.

Use today's adventure as a concrete roadmap of how to keep good soil in our lives. Help kids understand that they can turn to God for help when worries or problems threaten their faith. Help them see that God desires a close relationship with them—that's why he planted the seeds of faith in their hearts. Just think, you're the one today who's watering those seeds! Who knew you had such a green thumb!

TOUR GUIDE TIP
The experiences in this book have been designed for multi-age groups. Select from the experiences, or adapt them as needed for your kids.

DEPARTURE PRAYER (up to 5 minutes)

Gather kids together.

Say: **I've been enjoying exploring Jesus' parables with you. Today's parable will really grow on you—promise. But before we dig in, let's think about this for a minute. First, grab two partners.**

Have kids form trios. Give each trio a piece of paper and a pencil.

Say: **Okay, think about something important you've learned as you've grown to this point in your life. Maybe you've learned how to ride a bike, or how to play your favorite video game, or how to brush your teeth! After you've thought of something, tell your partners your idea.**

Then, together, come up with one thing that *all* three of you have

Items to Pack:
paper, pencils

learned and agree is important. When you've decided on one answer, have the oldest person in your group write the answer on your piece of paper.

Give groups a minute or two to discuss and write. Then have each group present its answer to everyone else. Thank kids for their ideas.

Say: **Wow! You've learned some really important things as you've grown! But think about this.**

Ask: • **What would your life be like if you hadn't learned how to do some of those important things? For example, what if you never learned to talk?**

• **Or what if you had crossed your arms and said, "Forget it—I don't want to learn how to spell"? How would your life be different?**

Say: **As we grow, we learn important skills. If you couldn't spell, you couldn't continue in school, you couldn't write your name, you couldn't read, and you couldn't text. It's important to keep learning.**

It's the same way with God. God has important things to teach us—things that will help our lives so much. But we have to be willing to listen. We have to be open to learning. That's what today's parable is all about.

Let's ask God to help us be open to learning something important today.

Form a circle with kids. Explain that you'll go around the circle, and each person can say the answer its trio thought of. You'll start and end the prayer.

Pray: **Dear God, thank you for loving us so much that you want to teach us. Help us be open to what you have to say. Help us learn important things from you—things more important than...** Go around the circle as kids say their trios' answers. Then close the prayer. **God, please help us *want* to learn from you. We ask in Jesus' name, amen.**

(15 minutes)
Tall Towers
Kids will build tall towers and learn they can grow in their relationship with and knowledge of God.

Items to Pack:
paper, rolls of masking tape

Have kids form new trios. (If you have lots of kids, form larger groups of equal numbers.) Give each group a stack of paper and a roll of masking tape.

Say: **Since today we're talking about learning and growing, I**

TOUR GUIDE TIP

Help kids form groups that include a variety of ages. Older kids love helping and guiding younger ones, and younger kids feel included and valued. Combined ages really do work!

FUN FACT At the time Jesus told this parable, the main crops in the area were dates, figs, and olives.

Items to Pack:

Bibles

challenge you to see how big your group can "grow" a tower, using only the supplies I gave you. You'll have five minutes to build the tallest tower possible. Ready? Go!

As kids work, encourage groups to make their towers as tall as possible. Offer help and ideas as needed. After five minutes, call time. Have groups admire each others' work.

Say: **You really got those towers growing!**

Ask: • **What was the biggest challenge of building your tower?**

• **What might have made building the tower easier?**

Say: **You seemed to have fun building your towers. But you were also learning along the way. You didn't have a lot to start with—just paper and tape—but you all built pretty cool towers.**

You know, you can grow in your relationship with God, just as you "grew" your tower. And you don't need a lot to get started. God plants the seeds of faith in you and helps the seeds grow. 🌑 **God wants to grow the seeds of faith planted in us. Your part is making sure your heart is the right kind of soil. I'll show you what I mean!**

STORY EXCURSION

(15 minutes)

Sowing Seeds

This experience will teach kids that God's Word needs fertile "soil" to grow in.

Open your Bible to Mark 4:1-20, and show kids the passage.

Say: **The parable we'll be exploring is often called the parable of the sower. Now, I don't mean the kind of sewer who sews clothes. I mean someone who sows seeds in the ground, like a farmer.**

Remember how I said this parable would grow on you? Get it? Grow? Hmm...*I* **thought that was funny. Anyway, I'll need your help as we *dig* into this passage. Get it? Dig?** Pause. **Really? You don't think that's funny? Oh well. Just follow my actions, Okay?**

Have everyone stand facing you. Tell the following paraphrase, leading kids in the suggested actions.

Say: **This is a parable that Jesus told about a farmer. One day the farmer was planting some seed for his crops.** Pretend to toss seed onto the ground from a bag you're holding. **Some of the seed fell on the road where people walked.** March in place. **The birds came and ate those seeds.** Flap your arms, caw like a crow, and lead kids quickly around the room one time.

The farmer sowed some more seed. Pretend to toss more seed. **Some of those seeds fell on shallow soil that had rocks underneath.** Pretend to dig into the ground with a shovel that hits solid rock. Grab your shoulder and say, "Ouch!" **The seeds sprouted quickly because the soil was shallow.** Crouch down and jump up quickly. **But the sun was hot.** Wipe your brow. **And since the plant didn't have deep roots in the shallow soil, it withered and died.** Pretend to wilt until you're crouching down again.

The farmer planted *more* seed! Pretend to toss more seed. **Now these seeds fell among the thorns that grew up around the plant and choked out the tender young plants.** Grab your throat and pretend to couch. **So those plants died, too.** Wilt into another crouch.

Finally, the farmer planted seed in nice, fertile soil. Pretend to toss more seed. **These seeds sprouted and grew and produced a crop that was 30, 60, even 100 times more than the seeds that had been planted by the farmer!** Crouch down, and slowly stand tall as you speak, ending with your arms reaching to the sky.

Say: **Wow! I *love* that parable! Let's dig into it a little more. And no, I don't expect you to laugh.** Have kids form four groups, and give each group a Bible. **In your group, you're going to discuss a few questions. When your group has come up with an answer, have the person wearing the most green quietly raise his or her hand. When every group has a hand raised, we'll compare answers. Here are the questions.**

Ask: • **In this parable, what do you think the seed the farmer was planting stands for?**

Wait until each group has a hand raised; then let each group give its answer.

Say: **Jesus told his disciples what he meant by this parable. Have the person wearing the most red read aloud Mark 4, verse 14 for your group.**

After each group has read the verse, continue. **Okay, so we know the seed is the Word of God. Some of the seed fell on the footpath, and the birds ate it.**

Ask: • **What do you think that means? Discuss in your group, and have the "green" person raise a hand when you have an answer.**

Continue the same process for the rest of the kinds of seeds—the seeds that spouted quickly, the seed choked by thorns, and the seed on fertile soil. Have each group give its answer for each kind of seed, but wait until after all have offered their opinions about all of the seeds to turn to the Bible.

Say: **This is kind of a mystery, isn't it? When you're not sure of an**

Encourage older kids to help younger readers.

answer, it's always best to turn to the Bible. Let's try it! I need seven volunteers to read from the Bible. (Or, if you have a smaller group, ask volunteers to read two or three verses.) Have the first volunteer read Mark 4:14, the second volunteer read verse 15, and so on until someone has read all the way through verse 20. Thank the volunteer readers.

When volunteers have finished reading the verses, ask:

• **What surprised you about the verses?**

• **What kinds of problems or worries in your life could keep your seeds of faith from growing?**

• **What can you do to make sure your seeds of faith have good soil to grow in?**

Say: **We know that the seed is God's Word, and it needs good soil to grow. We can make sure we have good soil by reading God's Word, by praying to God, and by asking him for help with our problems and worries. That way, the seeds of faith can grow and produce a good harvest in our lives.**

Ask: • **What do you think a good harvest in your life might look like?**

Say: **A good harvest is God's Word working in our lives. It's how we act after we read God's Word and accept it and believe it. God's Word plants seeds of faith in us, and the more we read it and pray, the more the seeds grow.** 🌑 **God wants to grow the seeds of faith planted in us. Let's see what that might look like.**

ADVENTURES IN GROWING

(10 minutes)

Good Soil Scenes

Kids will discover more about how to have "good soil" in their lives.

Items to Pack:
Bibles, 3-foot lengths of butcher paper or newsprint, crayons, colored markers, tape

Have kids stay in their groups, and be sure each group still has a Bible. Give each group a 3-foot sheet of butcher paper or newsprint, plus art supplies such as markers and crayons.

Say: **In your group, think about one thing you could do that would show that the seeds of faith are growing in the good soil of your life—an action that would show that God's Word is growing in your heart. Maybe it's an action that would show God's love to someone at school, like sitting with a new person at lunch. Or maybe it's an action where you help someone in your family, like taking out the** trash without being asked.

In your group, come up with an action you all like. Then work together to draw a picture of a person doing that action. We'll put the pictures together to form scenes of good soil and growing faith! You'll have about five minutes.

After five minutes, have each group present and explain its drawing. After each presentation, lead everyone in a round of applause. Then have kids help you hang the pictures on the wall, end-to-end, to create a mural showing scenes of good soil and growing faith!

Say: **Thanks for helping us discover how to produce good soil in our lives—soil that helps the seeds of faith grow. Before we end today, let's talk about how we can help the seeds of faith grow in others.**

SOUVENIRS

(10 minutes)
Seeds of Faith

Kids will see that they can help others grow closer to God.

SCENIC ROUTE

For extra fun, have each group silently act out its action before showing its picture. Let everyone guess the action before revealing the drawing.

Set out crayons, colored markers, scissors, transparent tape, and glue sticks. Give each person a copy of the "Seeds of Faith" handout.

Say: **Today we're learning that 🌑 God wants to grow the seeds of faith planted in us. And the cool thing is, we can help grow seeds of faith in others! Here's how.**

You can color your seed packet, and then cut it out. You'll glue the two sides together, colored sides facing out. But only glue the sides and bottom together so the top is still open.

After that, cut out the Bible verses—the seeds of faith. Put them inside the seed packet, fold the top down, and tape it closed.

And then for the most important part: Decide who you'll give your Seeds of Faith packet to. Think of someone you know who could use a little help growing closer to God. Write that person's name on the Seeds of Faith packet in the blank.

When everyone has finished, say: **Let's put your Seeds of Faith seed packets in your Travel Journals today as reminders that you can help others grow the seeds of faith. When we've finished our travels through the parables, you can give your seed packet to the person you thought of. Pray for that person this week.**

Items to Pack:
Bibles, copies of the "Seeds of Faith" handout from page 87, crayons, fine-tipped colored markers, scissors, glue sticks

Before we close, let's take a minute to thank God for planting seeds of faith in us, and for helping those seeds grow.

HOME AGAIN PRAYER

(10 minutes)

Give each person a white foam cup. Have kids decorate their cups and write their names on them.

Say: **Today we've been talking about how seeds need good soil to grow. Let's make something to help us remember that our lives need good spiritual soil so the seeds of faith can grow.**

Have kids each fill their cups about two-thirds full with potting soil. Drop in a few seeds and pat them down according to package directions. Mist with a little water.

Then gather kids in a circle with their finished cups.

Say: **Take your cups home and put them in a sunny window. Remember to mist them with water now and then, and soon you'll see the seeds you planted grow! Every time you look at your cup, remember that**  **God wants to grow the seeds of faith planted in us. Let's ask God to help us right now.**

Pray: **Dear Lord, thank you for planting seeds of faith in us. Help us to make sure our lives of full of good spiritual soil so those seeds can grow. In Jesus' name, amen.**

Items to Pack:

white foam cups, colored markers, potting soil, spoons, fast-growing grass or plant seeds, spray bottle of water set to "mist"

TOUR GUIDE TIP

Your local garden shop can suggest a fast-growing seed for your geographical area.

"Give all your worries and cares to God, for he cares about you." 1 Peter 5:7

"_____ , may God grow the seeds of faith into your life."

"But God showed his great love for us by sending Christ to die for us while we were still sinners." Romans 5:8

"_____ , may God grow the seeds of faith into your life."

"Faith is the confidence that what we hope for will actually happen." Hebrews 11:1a

"_____ , may God grow the seeds of faith into your life."

"For nothing is impossible with God." Luke 1:37

"_____ , may God grow the seeds of faith into your life."

The Parable of the Tower Builder

Pathway Point: God asks us to count the cost of being a disciple of Jesus.

Summary of Parable: A builder started to construct a tower, only to find that he'd failed to plan for what it would cost. The result was that he ended up building only a foundation before abandoning the project. (Luke 14:25-35)

Travel Itinerary

This parable is one that many kids—and many adults—are likely not to be familiar with. Perhaps that's because it's hard to talk about the cost of following Jesus. It's uncomfortable to acknowledge that there is a price for our faith. And it's unpopular to admit to kids that being a Christian isn't easy. But you can use this lesson as an *encouragement* to kids! Help them understand that even though walking with Jesus will be challenging, God is faithfully beside us through everything we face.

TOUR GUIDE TIP

The experiences in this book have been designed for multi-age groups. Select from the experiences, or adapt them as needed for your kids.

DEPARTURE PRAYER (up to 5 minutes)

Gather kids in a circle and say: **You all look like a pretty strong bunch of kids. I'll bet there are plenty of things in this room that would be easy for you to lift.**

Choose a few kids to lift objects in your classroom such as a chair, a Bible, or a small table.

Say: **And I'll bet that all of you can lift your finger!** Let kids demonstrate how they can lift their fingers easily. **In fact, you'd think I was crazy if I said you *couldn't* lift a finger...but it's true.**

Have kids place their palms together, as if in prayer. Then demonstrate how to roll your fingers in, so you have two fists "facing" each other (see illustration). Now, raise your ring fingers so they're touching each other.

Say: **Make sure your knuckles are touching each other, and then slowly try to lift your ring fingers apart.** Let kids try the challenge.

Then ask: • **Think of something in life that seemed easy, but when you tried it, it was hard. What made it hard?**

Share an experience from your own life, and then let kids share their stories.

Say: **Today we'll hear about something that some people in the Bible thought would be easy. Jesus challenged them to think about it in a new way. We'll see that 🌐 God asks us to count the cost of being a disciple of Jesus. Before we start, put your hands back together, with your ring fingers extended—just like we did earlier.**

Pause, and then lead children in prayer. Pray: **Loving God, we know that following Jesus is an important and wonderful thing. We also know that there are challenges when we decide to follow Jesus. Help us listen and learn as we explore your Word. Show us how we can be faithful disciples of Jesus. In Jesus' name, amen.**

(10 minutes)

Bakery Blues

Help kids discover the disappointment that can come when we don't plan and prepare adequately.

Say: **Before we get started, I have to say—I'm hungry! Let's have a snack. Better yet, let's make a warm, yummy cake. I *love* the smell of a cake baking, don't you?**

Ask: • **What do you like best about cake?**

Say: **Oh, I'm getting even hungrier! And I brought in this boxed cake mix, so it'll be a snap.** Let a child open the mix, and ask another child to carefully pour the mix into the bowl. Another child can read the box to tell you how much water to add. Let another child add the right amount of water.

Ask: • **What do I do next?**

Have a child read the rest of the ingredients needed. Say: **Hmmm. Well, I don't have any of those ingredients. I guess I didn't think about that. And even if I did, I didn't think about bringing a spoon to mix it all up. Um, or a pan to put it in.**

Set the wet cake mix in the middle of the circle.

Ask: • **How do you feel about missing out on our warm, yummy cake?**

• **If I wanted to have cake, what should I have done before we met today?**

Say: **I didn't plan ahead, did I? I didn't read the directions or gather the right supplies. And now we're all feeling sad, disappointed, and hungry. I guess I didn't plan or prepare very well.**

Items to Pack:
a cake mix, water, a bowl, a measuring cup

TOUR GUIDE TIP

We've kept this activity simple by just using a boxed cake mix. However, you can make this experience more elaborate by bringing in half of the ingredients needed to make a cake from scratch.

Ask: • **When are times when *you* have to plan or prepare things ahead of time?**

Kids might consider things like packing for a sleepover or vacation, or working on a big project for school.

Say: **Did you know that God wants us to plan and prepare our hearts to follow Jesus? ◗ God asks us to count the cost of being a disciple of Jesus. Let's take a look at how Jesus challenged people to think about what it would be like to be his follower.**

STORY EXCURSION

(20 minutes)

Count the Cost

Kids will decide whether or not they're willing to give something up as they listen to this parable about counting the cost of following Jesus.

Say: **As I share this true story from God's Word, we're going to play a game...if you want to. Here's the deal. If you want to play, I'll give you a handful of pennies. Every time you hear me say a certain word in the story, you have to give me one of your pennies. You'll get any pennies you have left over at the end of the Scripture passage. But if you run out, you have to give me something else you have. Maybe your shoe or a barrette or something in your pocket. I may give it back...but I may not. So first you have to decide if you're in or out.**

Let kids choose. If some don't want to risk playing, that's okay. They can just listen and observe. Distribute pennies to everyone who is participating.

Open your Bible to Luke 14:25-35. Say: **Listen to this passage from Luke 14. Every time you hear the word *you*, give me a penny. Remember, if you run out of pennies, you have to bring me something else.**

You can read the passage from your own Bible, or from the text below. If you read from your own passage, be sure that you've counted the number of times the word *you* is mentioned and give children a few less pennies than that number. As you read, pause after you say the word *you*.

"A large crowd was following Jesus. He turned around and said to them, If you want to be my disciple, you must hate everyone else by comparison—your father and mother, wife and children, brothers and sisters—yes, even your own life. Otherwise, you cannot be my disciple. And if you do not carry your own cross and follow me, you cannot be my disciple. But don't begin until you count the cost. For who would begin construction of a building without first calculating the cost to see if there is enough money to finish it? Otherwise you might complete only the foundation before running out of money, and then everyone would laugh at you. They would say, 'There's the person who started that building and couldn't afford to finish it!' Or what king would go to war against another king without first sitting down with his counselors to discuss whether his army of 10,000 could defeat the 20,000 soldiers marching against him? And if he can't, he will send a delegation to discuss terms of peace while the enemy is still far away. So you cannot become my disciple without giving up everything you own.

Salt is good for seasoning. But if it loses its flavor, how do you make it salty again? Flavorless salt is good neither for the soil nor for the manure pile. It is thrown away. Anyone with ears to hear should listen and understand!"

Say: **At the beginning of the story, I gave you a choice—you could choose to play or not. Turn to two friends and talk about this:**

• **Why did *you* choose to play or not to play?**

Allow a minute for trios to discuss the question. Then ask a few kids to share their responses with the larger group.

Ask: • **What did this game cost you?**

• **How did you feel about giving up those things?**

Say: **At the beginning of this Bible passage, there was a huge crowd following Jesus. Jesus *was* kind of famous! People wanted to be his special friends, or disciples. But Jesus knew that his disciples would go through hard things. In your trio, think of three things that it *costs*—things you might have to give up or ways you might have to change—to be a follower of Jesus today.**

Let kids talk for a minute; then take reports from each group.

Ask: • **Why do you think God asks us to count the cost of being a disciple of Jesus?**

Say: **Jesus told about a man who started a building but didn't have materials to finish it.** Have kids stand to pretend they're half-built buildings.

FUN FACT In Jesus' day, people had to work hard to make good, pure salt—which usually came from the Dead Sea. When the salt mixed with sand or other impurities, it lost flavor. The people listening to Jesus would understand that Jesus wanted their lives to be pure—like salt—without "impurities" that took away their zeal for God.

Say: **Now squat a little so you're halfway between standing and sitting.** Let kids remain in this pose for a *long* two minutes.

Then ask: • **How do you half-built buildings feel?**

• **How would you feel if you'd been the builder of the half-built building and people laughed at you?**

Let kids sit down. Then say: **Jesus wanted strong followers—followers who would stay faithful even when they felt tired, discouraged, or even embarrassed. He had important work for his followers, so he wanted people who would stick with him to the end and not give up.**

Jesus also talked about salt being salty. Today we like salty foods, but in Bible times, salt was super important because it kept food from going bad.

People needed salt in order to have good, wholesome food.

Ask: • **How do you think Jesus' disciples were like salt?**

Say: ◑ **God wants us to count the cost of being a disciple of Jesus. God knows that it can be challenging...that sometimes you have to give up things. But when we make the decision to follow Jesus, God gives *us* strength and hope and peace.**

Hand back kids' belongings, along with a hug or high five. Encourage each child with a phrase such as, "[Child's name], stay strong as you follow Jesus."

ADVENTURES IN GROWING

(10 minutes)

Missing Chairs

Use this game to help kids think of practical ways to show that they're God-followers in everyday life.

Items to Pack:
CD player, a CD of upbeat music, 1 chair for every child

This activity is similar to musical chairs. Make a circle of chairs, with the seats facing out.

Say: **In the Bible passage, people wanted to follow Jesus because they thought he was famous and cool. Maybe they thought it would be easy...or even make them famous! The story Jesus told them showed that ◑ God wants us to count the cost of being a disciple of Jesus. When you follow Jesus, *you're* a disciple, too! Let's see what that looks like today.**

In this game, I'll play music while you walk around the chairs. When the music stops, if you don't have a chair you'll get to help us think of what it means to be a disciple of Jesus today. I'll call out a

place and I want you to tell me how you can show that you're Jesus' follower at that place. Then I'll take away a chair.

Play the game and guide kids in exploring what it means to be a disciple—a follower or friend of Jesus—at school, at home, on the playground, while they play sports, while they're on the Internet, and when they're with their friends.

When one person remains, gather kids and say: **Even though it might be hard to show that you're Jesus' special friend, God will always be with you and give you the strength to follow Jesus. I'm so thankful for all of you faithful followers!**

SOUVENIRS

(10 minutes)

Kids will create a reminder that following Jesus sometimes means putting him before other things that we love.

Hand each child a photocopy of the "Count the Cost" handout. Direct kids to think of things that they love and then to write each of those things on a coin. Say: ◗ **God asks us to count the cost of being Jesus' disciple. Sometimes that means that the things we love have to be less important than Jesus. Jesus said that we have to love him more than anything. As you glue foil over these coins, pray that God will help you to put Jesus first and be his faithful disciple every day.**

You may want to play reflective music as kids cut out foil "coins" and glue them over the words they wrote on their handouts. Kids can add these sheets to their Travel Journals.

> **Items to Pack:**
> 1 photocopy of the "Count the Cost" handout on page 95 for each child, markers, glue, kid-friendly scissors, aluminum foil, CD player, CD of reflective music

HOME AGAIN PRAYER

(5 minutes)

This active, guided prayer will allow kids to move as they express their devotion to Jesus.

Say: **Jesus' followers were called disciples. They literally followed Jesus from town to town, but they also stuck with him as friends. They learned from him so they could teach others. As we play a simple game of Follow the Leader, I'll lead us in prayer. We'll ask God for help in being Jesus' disciples.**

Have kids line up. Stand where all kids can see you. Lead them in taking a step forward, and then pray: **God, it can be hard to give all of ourselves to you as we follow Jesus. We give you our words. Help our words be** truthful and helpful, filled with your love. In Jesus' name, amen.

Lead kids in taking another step forward, and then pray: **Lord, we give you our actions. Help us to act like people who are friends with Jesus...even when we want to do things that we know aren't right. We look to you for the strength to choose what pleases you. In Jesus' name, amen.**

Lead kids in taking another step forward, and then pray: **God, we give you our thoughts. We want to think like followers of Jesus. Help us to keep our thoughts on things that please you and honor you. Help us to guard our minds so that they're filled with your love. In Jesus' name, amen.**

Count the Cost

JOURNEY 11

The Parable of the Feast That the Invited Guests Refused to Attend

Pathway Point: 🌐 God wants us in heaven with him.

Summary of Parable: A man plans a great banquet. He sends invitations to his prospective guests along with the promise that he will send a messenger when all is ready. After the feast is prepared, the host sends a servant to give notice to those invited that all is ready. All invited guests send back lame excuses for not attending. The banquet host then sends the servant to the highways and hedges to bring in the lame, maimed, and blind to celebrate with him instead of those who refused to attend. (Luke 14:12-24)

Travel Itinerary

From an early age, kids discover the fun of being invited...to a party, a sleepover, or just to hang out at a friend's house. They also discover too soon the pain of being left out. What a joy to realize that God invites *all* of us into a relationship with him that will last forever!

Use today's lesson to remind kids of God's incredible love for them—a love so great that he's preparing an incredible place in heaven for each and every one.

TOUR GUIDE TIP

The experiences in this book have been designed for multi-age groups. Select from the experiences, or adapt them as needed for your kids.

DEPARTURE PRAYER — (up to 5 minutes)

Items to Pack:
party decorations such as balloons, streamers, and tablecloths; paper plates, napkins

Gather kids and say: **I'm so glad you're here today! We have an exciting Bible story to explore today, and *you're* going to help set the stage for a big celebration.** Ask: • **What things do *you* do when you're getting ready to have a party or celebration at home?**

Say: **The parable we're exploring is about a party called a banquet—a big, fancy feast. Let's decorate our room for a party!**

Set out the supplies and let kids decorate your room for a party. Kids can inflate balloons and hang them up, twist streamers together and hang them in doorways, and put a tablecloth on the table. When the room is ready, gather kids around the table.

Say: **There's something missing.** Hold up the paper plates. **There's a place for each of you at our table. Today we'll be talking about heaven—an incredible place that *God* is preparing for *us!* 🌐 God** wants us in heaven with him. **Let's start our time together by thanking God for making a special place for each one of us in heaven.**

Hand each child a plate. As kids take turns setting their plate at the table, have them pray a short prayer of thanks. Close by praying: **God, it's incredible to think that you love us enough to make a place for each and every one of us in heaven with you. Open our eyes so that we can better understand your loving plans. In Jesus' name, amen.**

CHOKING HAZARD—Children under 8 yrs. can choke or suffocate on uninflated or broken balloons. Adult supervision required. Keep uninflated balloons from children. Discard broken balloons at once. Balloons may contain latex.

(10 minutes)

You're Invited...

Kids will make invitations to a "dream" party, and then explore what it feels like when people can't come.

Gather kids away from the party table.

Ask: • **What are some occasions for having a party?**

• **Who do you usually invite to a party?**

Say: **It's really fun to plan a party—*and* to get a party invitation.** Hold up the "You're Invited" invitations. **Take a minute and fill in the blanks and decorate these party invitations. You can plan any kind of party you want. Dream big! As you plan, think about how much fun you and your friends and family will have at your party.**

Items to Pack:
a photocopy of the "You're Invited" invitations from page 102 for each child, pens or pencils, markers, CD of upbeat music, CD player

Set out pens and markers and give each child an invitation. Play upbeat music for about five minutes while kids create their invitations. Then form a circle and say: **Pass your invitation to the left while the music plays. When I stop the music, look over the invitation you have and then find the person who invited you to his or her party. Then I want you to make up a weird or ridiculous reason for *not* coming to the party. Ready?** Play upbeat music for a few seconds, and then turn it off. After kids have exchanged excuses, gather kids together again and ask for a few of the strange excuses they heard.

Ask: • **How would you feel if *no one* came to your party?**

Say: **In today's parable, Jesus used the example of someone who planned a party that no one came to. We'll discover that 🌐 God wants us in heaven with him.**

Gather the invitations to use in the next part of the lesson.

FUN FACT

In Bible times, people usually sent *two* invitations to a feast: one as a "save the date" announcement, then another one when the banquet was ready. The host expected attendance from those who accepted the first invitation.

STORY EXCURSION

(20 minutes)

The Parable of the Great Feast

Guide kids in acting out this parable in a meaningful way, exploring how people say "no" to God.

Open your Bible to Luke 14:12, and show kids the passage. Say: **One Sabbath day, Jesus went to have dinner at an important Pharisee's house. While he was there, Jesus noticed how everyone wanted the best place at the table. So Jesus told the host that it's better to invite people who can't pay you back—people who aren't worried about impressing you. Jesus said that in heaven, "God will reward you for inviting those who could not repay you." So that got everyone thinking about heaven. In fact, one guy called out, "It's going to be great to feast with God in heaven!" And that was when Jesus told this story.**

Hold the invitations and have kids scatter around the room. Stand near the party table kids prepared earlier.

Say: **A man prepared a great feast and sent out many invitations.** Walk around the room and hand a few kids invitations. Then walk back to the table. **When the banquet was ready, he sent his servant to tell the guests, 'Come, the banquet is ready.' But they all began making excuses. One said, 'I have just bought a field and must inspect it. Please excuse me.'** Walk to one child and tear up his or her invitation. **That person didn't want to come.** Walk to another child. **Another said, 'I have just bought five pairs of oxen, and I want to try them out. Please excuse me.'** Tear up that person's invitation. **Guess he didn't want to come, either.** Walk to another child. **Another said, 'I now have a wife, so I can't come.'** Tear up that person's invitation.

Continue to move to everyone you gave an invitation to, taking their invitations and tearing them. **Everyone that the man had invited to the feast had some excuse for not coming.** Take all the torn invitations and put them in a pile.

Continue: **The servant returned and told his master what they had said. His master was furious and said, 'Go quickly into the streets and alleys of the town and invite the poor,** (hand a child an invitation) **the crippled** (hand a few more children invitations), **the blind** (continue handing out invitations), **and the lame.' After the servant had done this, he** reported, 'There is still room for more.' So this master said, 'Go out into the country lanes and behind the hedges and urge anyone you find to come, so that the house will be full. Hand out all of the invitations, • then direct kids who have invitations to come and gather around the table. For none of those I first invited will get even the smallest taste of my banquet.'

Ask: **Why did the man in the story invite the poor, crippled, and lame to his feast?**

• **If the man in the story represents God, and the banquet is heaven, why do you think Jesus told this story?**

Say:  **God wants us in heaven with him. Like the man in the story, God has planned and created something** *incredible* **for those who follow and love him! Heaven is so amazing that God wants everyone to be there. The doors are wide open! Let's bring our friends who said "no" so they can join our celebration.**

Have a few kids gathered near the table go and bring back the kids whose invitations you tore up.

ADVENTURES IN GROWING

(10 minutes)

I'll Be There!

Kids will have fun with a party game that also gets them thinking about how people today make excuses to God.

Items to Pack:
a photocopy of the "Partygoers" handout from page 102 for each child, tape, scissors, pens, a bandanna or other cloth to use as a blindfold, a whiteboard or newsprint, markers

Before kids arrive, cut apart the paper figures on the "Partygoers" handout so each child has a figure.

Say: **In the parable, a man prepared a feast.** Draw a large table on a whiteboard, or piece of newsprint. **He invited many of his friends.** Hand each child one of the figures. **But the people made up excuses for not coming. Suddenly, other things were more important. Remember, Jesus told this story to remind the Jewish leaders that**  **God wants us in heaven with him. So think about this quietly.**

Ask: • **What things can seem more important than spending time with God?**

Pause while kids think. Direct kids to turn the paper figure over and complete this sentence on the back of the paper, "I'd like to spend time with God, but..." Explain that no one will look at what they write.

Say:  **God wants us in heaven with him, but all of our excuses take us away from God.** Hand each child a piece of tape and let kids attach the tape to the top of their paper figures.

Play a game that's similar to "Pin the Tail on the Donkey." Take turns blindfolding children, spinning them around, and then having them try to attach their figures to the picture of the table. When everyone has had a turn, point to the picture with the partygoers and ask: • **How does this remind you of the parable Jesus told?**

• **How do you think God feels when he sees so many people make excuses to not spend time with him?**

Say: **God wants us in heaven with him. And God wants to spend time with us right *now*, too! Let's live lives that show God, "I'll be there! Count me in!"**

SOUVENIRS →

(10 minutes)

Imagine That

Let kids take time to imagine and express what *they* think heaven will be like.

Say: **Heaven is going to be an incredible celebration—and God wants you there! The Bible gives us clues about what heaven will be like—streets of gold, full of joy and light, jewels, trees, and people who love God. No sadness, tears, or pain. I don't know about you, but there's no way I want to miss *that*!**

Have kids take their "Partygoer" from the previous activity and tape it to a sheet of paper. Then have kids draw a scene of heaven around their person. Kids can imagine what heaven might be like, or check out Bible passages like Revelation 21:3-4, 10-12; 22:1-2, 5. Or, children might just draw themselves at a feast like the one Jesus described in the parable.

Play reflective worship music while kids design their pictures. Talk about what *you* think heaven will be like, and remind kids that **God wants us in heaven with him.** When kids finish, they can add their pictures to their Travel Journals.

Items to Pack:
paper, markers, CD of worship music, CD player, tape

(10 minutes)

Enjoy a party with kids and celebrate the heavenly banquet God is preparing for his followers.

Motion to the party table the kids set up in the Departure Prayer.

Ask: **What's missing from this table?**

Bring out whatever treat you prepared for kids, and set it on the table.

Say: **We started our journey today by preparing for a party—just as God is preparing something incredible in heaven for us. You had to wait a while for this celebration—just as we all have to wait to see what God has in store for us in heaven. But now it's time to celebrate! As I close our time in prayer, you'll hear a place where you can say your name. We'll go around the circle and you can each say your name during that part of the prayer.**

Join hands around the table and pray.

Pray: **God, we can only imagine the incredible things you've prepared for us in heaven. Thank you most of all that you love us enough to want each of us there with you. Thank you for preparing heaven for everyone here...** Begin by saying your name, • then let each child take a turn saying his or her name. When everyone has said a name, close by saying: **Help us to always put you first as we anticipate coming to *your* party in heaven. In Jesus' name, amen.**

Enjoy a party with your class!

**TOUR
GUIDE
TIP**

Some children have food allergies that can be dangerous. Know your children, and consult with parents about allergies their children may have. Also, read food labels carefully, as hidden ingredients can cause allergy-related problems.

You're Invited

To a party for _____!
Your Name

We'll eat lots of _____ ,
Food

play games like _____ ,
Game

and listen to music from _____!
Name of a band or a movie

Oh, and _____ will even be around!
Name of a famous person

I can't wait to see you there!

Partygoers

The Parable of the Persistent Widow

Pathway Point: God wants us to keep praying, no matter what.

Summary of Parable: A widow pleads repeatedly to a judge for justice. The judge sends her away time and again. The widow perseveres. Finally, the judge relents and grants the pleas of the widow, not because she was right, but because she persevered. (Luke 18:1-8)

Travel Itinerary

The kids in your ministry may not have yet discovered the truth that God's timing isn't our timing. That's a lesson most adults still struggle to accept! Guide kids in realizing that God wants us to be persistent in our prayers...not to wear him out like the judge in this parable, but to grow in our faith in and love for him. Use this lesson to remind kids that God is always listening, so we can pray without ceasing.

TOUR GUIDE TIP

The experiences in this book have been designed for multi-age groups. Select from the experiences, or adapt them as needed for your kids.

DEPARTURE PRAYER (up to 5 minutes)

Gather kids and welcome them. Ask kids to complete this sentence:

I never get tired of...

Be sure to complete the sentence for yourself, too! When everyone has shared, say: **We all have things we *love* to do—things we could do again and again and again. But sometimes we kind of wear out, even doing something we like. Let me show you what I mean.**

Turn on upbeat music and have kids stand up and start jumping up and down. Say: **Keep on jumping until you get tired. When you get tired, you can sit down.** After a few minutes (or when all kids are sitting), turn off the music and ask: **• I thought kids *loved* to be active and move around! What happened?**

Say: **Believe it or not, we can even get tired of doing something we like. Today we're going to talk about prayer—something that's not hard to do, but something that we often kind of give up on. We'll discover that** **God wants us to keep praying, no matter what.**

Have kids join hands. Pray: **Loving God, we're so thankful that you**

Items to Pack:
CD player, CD of upbeat music

want to hear us. Guide us as we learn more about prayer and how we can come to you again and again. Help us to listen and learn so that we can know you better. In Jesus' name, amen.

(10 minutes)

Back and Forth

Use this experience to help kids realize that prayer is a two-way conversation between God and us.

Items to Pack:

1 ball for every pair of kids

Say: **Let's get to know each other a little better. We'll go around the circle and you can tell us something about a good friend you have. Tell that person's name and one thing you like about that person.**

Begin by sharing about a friend of yours; then go around the circle and let each person share. Then ask: • **How do you get to know someone?**

• **How do you get to know God?**

Say: **We have an amazing God who wants to spend time with us—just like you spend time with your friends. We can get to know God through prayer. Lots of times we think of prayer as a list of things to say, but prayer is more like a conversation. Let me show you what I mean.**

Form pairs and give each pair a ball. Have partners stand about 10 feet apart. Direct the person with the longest hair to start by asking his or her partner a question such as, "What's your favorite food?" or "Where did you go on your last vacation?" Then the person will toss the ball. The partner will catch the ball, answer the question, and then ask a new question before tossing the ball back.

Let kids play for about five minutes; then collect the balls and have kids sit down.

Ask: • **What did you learn about your partner?**

• **How is prayer like or unlike this activity?**

• **How could you make your prayers *more* like this experience?**

Say: ◐ **God wants us to keep praying, no matter what. When we see prayer as more of a conversation, it's easier to come to God every day—no matter what else is going on in our lives. Let's see how Jesus showed people the power of prayer through a parable.**

STORY EXCURSION

(15 minutes)

The Persistent Widow

Kids will have fun acting out this story, giving you their "burdens" just as the persistent widow did to the judge.

Open your Bible to Luke 18:1-8, and show kids the words. Say: **Jesus loved using stories to make a point. Sometimes he explained what the story meant, and sometimes he wanted people to keep thinking about it and figure it out themselves. This parable is super clear! Listen to these words from Luke 18.**

"One day Jesus told his disciples a story to show that they should always pray and never give up."

Ask: • **Why would Jesus want us to always pray and never give up?**

Give a handful of stones to each child and direct kids to hold the rocks, not set them on the floor. Stand up and hold the bucket in front of you.

Say: **This is the story Jesus told.**

In a certain city there was a judge who didn't fear God and didn't care about people. There was also a widow in that city. Now, in Bible times, a widow was most likely poor and had a low place in society. She didn't have a husband to care for or protect her. This widow came to the judge and said, "Give me justice in this dispute I'm having."

Bring me a rock to represent the widow bringing her request to the judge. Pause while kids plunk rocks into the bucket you're holding. When everyone has added a rock, continue: **The judge ignored the widow...I mean, she was just a poor, lowly widow, right? But she came back with her same request.** Let kids each add another rock to the bucket. **And she came again.** Kids may add another rock to the bucket. **And again!** Let kids bring up any remaining rocks they have.

Say: **Finally, the judge said, "I may not fear God and I sure don't care about people, but this woman is driving me crazy!** Show kids how heavy the bucket is and how weary you are from holding it. **I'm going to see that she gets justice because she's wearing me out with her constant requests!"**

Jesus told his friends to learn a lesson from the story of the judge. Even the judge gave a fair decision in the end...won't God do the same for the people he loves and has chosen? Then Jesus said, "I tell you,

FUN FACT

Jesus had a reason to include a widow as a character in his parable. Widows were defenseless in New Testament times. Women not only relied upon a husband or other family member to provide for their physical needs, but to represent them in court.

God will grant justice to them quickly! But when the Son of Man returns, how many will he find on the earth who have faith?"

Set down your heavy load and ask: • **How is God like or unlike the judge in this story?**

• **Why would people give up praying?**

Say: **When Jesus told this story, God's people didn't have a leader or king of their own. They didn't feel like things were fair for them. Jesus wanted to remind them not to give up—that God still heard them and loved them just as much as ever. And today, 🌑 God wants us to keep praying, no matter what.**

Ask: • **How did it feel to get rid of those rocks as I told the story?**

• **How is that like the feeling when you pray about something?**

Say: **This story doesn't mean God will do whatever we ask. God knows the bigger picture and sometimes his plans are different than what we'd like. But it *does* feel good to give our heartaches, sadness, frustration—those heavy things—to a God who listens to and cares for us. That's why 🌑 God wants us to keep praying, no matter what.**

◆ **ADVENTURES IN GROWING**

(10 minutes)

Pray Every Day

Use this experience to help kids plan to put their requests before God each and every day.

Items to Pack:

photocopies of a wall calendar month for each child, pens

Before this lesson, make copies of a basic wall calendar that has the current month on it. If it's mid-month, photocopy next month's calendar as well.

Say: **Sometimes we stop praying because we just forget or get busy. So let's make a cool calendar to remind us that 🌑 God wants us to keep praying, no matter what.**

Give each person a calendar and ask kids to think of something they'd like to talk with God about each day. Kids might have a prayer request for healing, for their parents, for a problem at school, or even something they'd like to thank God for every day. Ask kids to write or draw that prayer—even just a word about that prayer—on every square of the calendar.

Say: **For the next month, you'll be like the widow in the story. Bring your request or your praise to God every day, no matter what. As you see God respond to your prayer, write or draw that response on the back.**

Ask: • **How might God respond as you pray every day?**

Allow time for kids to respond. Say: **God may answer your prayer with a yes. God may tell you why he's saying no. God may give you the peace that he's in control. God may send people into your life who show you something new about God. Or, God may respond through something you read in the Bible. Have faith that God *will* respond! Because ● God wants us to keep praying, no matter what.**

SOUVENIRS →

(10 minutes)

Kids will make a reminder of what it means to pray without giving up.

Items to Pack:
a copy of the "Infinity" handout from page 109 for each child, markers or pens

Show kids the "Infinity" handout. Point out how the shape doesn't really have a beginning or end.

Say: **This is the sign for "infinity." Infinity is something that goes on forever without ending. ● God wants us to keep praying, no matter what. That means we always take time to come to God—with requests, praises, even to listen quietly.**

Give kids each a pen or marker, and let them write a prayer in the lines of the infinity sign. Remind kids that they don't have to ask God for something. Kids can offer praises, thanksgiving, or just acknowledge who God is.

When kids finish, let them add their "Infinity" papers to their Travel Journals.

HOME AGAIN PRAYER

(up to 5 minutes)

Guide kids in an experience to help them consider what they can talk with God about.

Form a circle. Hand each child four of the rocks from the bucket and set the bucket in the middle of the circle.

Say: **Prayer is more than just us asking God for stuff. Let's use these rocks to see what prayer can be.**

Lead kids in the following experience. This will be a quiet, reflective time.

Pray: **God, we love you so much. We praise you for being the mighty, powerful, gentle, loving God who made us. We come before you with our praise.** Guide kids in placing one rock in the bucket.

Pray: **God, you are so perfect...but we're not. Lord, we sin—we do wrong things that keep us from a good relationship with you. Please**

Items to Pack:
large bucket of stones from Story Excursion activity

forgive us as we silently tell you the wrong things we've done. Guide kids in placing another rock in the bucket.

Pray: **God, you've given us so much to be thankful for. Thank you for strong, healthy bodies and minds. For families who love us. For clean air and water. Thank you that you loved us enough to send your son to earth. We love you, God.**

Direct kids to put a third rock into the bucket.

Pray: **God, we do have things on our hearts—needs that we have, questions we want to ask. Hear us as we silently lay our request at your feet. Thank you for hearing us.** Direct kids to put their last rock in the bucket.

Pray: **In Jesus' name, amen.**

Infinity Symbol

JOURNEY 13

The Parable of the Good Samaritan

Pathway Point:  God wants us to care for others.

> **Summary of Parable:** A Jewish man unwisely travels alone to Jericho along a dangerous road, where robbers beat him nearly to death and take all of his possessions. Two honorable religious leaders pass him by. A Samaritan, a member of a group despised by Jews, ignored their religious and political differences, and soothed his wounds with olive oil and wine and bandaged them. Then he put the man on his own donkey and took him to an inn, where he took care of him. The Samaritan paid for the inn out of his own pocket. Without doubt, the Samaritan man saved the Jewish man's life. (Luke 10:25-37)

Travel Itinerary

It's not terribly difficult to care for people we love, is it? Or to care for our friends. But what about people we don't especially like? (C'mon, admit it, there's probably *someone*.) People who aren't nice to us? People we don't agree with?

God wants us to care for others, but he doesn't differentiate. In fact, in the parable of the good Samaritan, Jesus throws out preconceived opinions and dislikes. The Jews didn't like the Samaritans (and vice versa), but only the Samaritan in the parable stopped to help the injured man.

Use this session to help kids understand that God wants us to show love and mercy and compassion for everyone. Isn't that what Jesus did for us?

| **DEPARTURE PRAYER** | (up to 5 minutes) |

Bring kids together.

Say: **Today we'll explore another parable that Jesus told. It's got to do with caring for others—or not! First, let's discover what it means to care for others.**

Set out a variety of child-friendly magazines. Have kids form trios, and let trios quickly look through the magazines to find examples of people who care for others. Kids might find pictures or mention of doctors, nurses, teachers, firefighters, parents, and grandparents.

TOUR GUIDE TIP

The experiences in this book have been designed for multi-age groups. Select from the experiences, or adapt them as needed for your kids.

Items to Pack:
a variety of child-friendly magazines

After a few minutes, call time. Go around the room and let each trio tell one example they found, without repeating another trio's example. Keep going until no one has a new idea to add.

Ask: • **What did all of these examples have in common?**

• **Why do you think people care for each other?**

• **Who in your life cares for you?**

Say: **God loves us and he is our ultimate caregiver. He puts people in our lives who care for us and show us his love. And** **God wants us to care for others. Let's explore that idea.**

(15 minutes)

Care-for-Me Tag

Kids will decide whether or not to show caring during a game of Tag.

Items to Pack:
none

Say: **To get started, we're going to play a game of Tag. In this game, I'll choose someone to be "It," who will chase the rest of you. If It is about to tag you, you can call out, "Care!" Then It can decide whether to show caring or not. If It decides not to show caring, he or she can tag you and you'll have to sit down. If It does show caring, you'll become the new It.**

When everyone understands the rules, choose a child to be It. Play several rounds, making sure each child gets a turn to be It. After the game, have kids discuss these questions.

Ask: • **When you were It, how did you decide whether to show caring or not?**

• **If someone showed you caring, did you show caring to the next person? Why or why not?**

• **How did the choice to show caring or not affect the game?**

Say: **Whether to show caring was kind of a silly choice in our game. But it's an important choice in real life.** **God wants us to care for others. Jesus tells us more in this parable about someone who** *really* **needed a little care!**

Items to Pack:

Bibles

(15 minutes)

Are You My Neighbor?

This experience will teach kids that God wants us to care for other people, no matter who they are.

Open your Bible to Luke 10:25-37, and show kids the passage.

Say: **Today's parable is sometimes known as the parable of the good Samaritan. I'll need your help to tell what happened. But first let me give you a little background. One day an expert in religious law tried to trick Jesus by asking how to get eternal life. Jesus asked him what the law of Moses said. So the man said you had to love God and love your neighbor as yourself. Then he tried to trick Jesus again by asking, "And who is my neighbor?" Jesus answered by telling this parable.**

Ask: • **But real quickly before we get to the parable, let me ask you: Who is *your* neighbor?**

Let kids call out their answers.

Say: **Keep those answers in mind. We'll come back to them after we learn more about this parable! Here's what Jesus said. One day a Jewish man was traveling from Jerusalem to Jericho.**

Choose an outgoing boy to be the Jewish traveler. Explain that the rest of the kids will act together as they assume the other roles in the parable. Have the traveler and the "crowd" perform whatever actions they hear you describe for their roles. Pause where indicated to give kids time to react.

Say: **The Jewish man walked down the road, carrying his bag and whistling a tune.** Pause. **He knew that this road could be dangerous, so he kept looking back over his shoulder.** Pause. **Suddenly he heard a noise, and he stopped and looked around.** Pause.

Suddenly, a bunch of bandits jumped out of the bushes! Have everyone else pretend to jump out of bushes by the road. **The bandits surrounded the traveler.** Pause. **The traveler was so scared that his legs were shaking!** Pause.

Now I don't want you to actually do what the bandits did. Just pretend with your hands in the air, okay? The bandits took the traveler's clothes and pushed him and hit him. Pause. **Then they left him half dead by the side of the road, and they ran away.** Pause.

The poor traveler lay there by the side of the road, moaning and

FUN FACT

Samaritans were considered a low class of people by the Jews since Samaritans had intermarried with non-Jews and did not keep all the laws. Therefore, Jews would have nothing to do with them.

TOUR GUIDE TIP

It's fine to choose a girl to be the Jewish traveler. Just make sure she's not wearing a dress, as she'll be lying on the floor.

groaning. Pause. **Just then, a priest came walking along.** Have everyone in the large group walk in place. **The priest was brushing lint from his royal robes.** Pause. **The priest shielded his eyes from the sun and saw the man lying by the road.** Pause. **But instead of helping, he crossed to the other side of the road and walked past.** Pause.

The poor man was still moaning and groaning. Pause. **Then came a man who worked in the Temple, which was like the church.** Have kids in the large group walk in place. **He was smoothing his hair and fixing his hat.** Pause. **He shielded his eyes and saw the traveler lying by the road.** Pause. **But he crossed the road and walked past, too.** Pause.

The poor traveler was still lying there, moaning and groaning. Pause. **Then came along a hated Samaritan.** Walk in place. **Jews didn't like Samaritans because they didn't worship God the same way the Jews did.** Cross your arms over your chest. **But the Samaritan saw the poor traveler and went over to him.** Have the large group approach the traveler.

He felt compassion for the traveler, and soothed his wounds with oil and bandaged them. Pause as kids pretend to wrap the traveler in bandages.

Then he put the traveler on his own donkey. Pause. **He took him to an inn and took care of him. He fed him.** Pause. **He gave him something to drink.** Pause. **He patted his head.** Pause.

The next day, the Samaritan gave the innkeeper some money. Pause. **He said he had to go, but if it cost more to take care of the traveler, he'd come back with more money. Then the traveler and Samaritan waved goodbye to each other.** Pause.

Lead a round of applause for everyone's participation. Then gather kids together on the floor.

Ask: **• Which of the three men who came along would you call a neighbor to the poor traveler? Why?**

• What do you think Jesus is trying to tell us in this parable?

• How does this parable affect your definition of neighbor?

Say: **The people who heard Jesus tell this parable were surprised. They didn't like Samaritans, but it was only the Samaritan who actually acted like a neighbor to the poor traveler.** ◗**God wants us to care for others—no matter who they are. Let's see what that means for our lives.**

SCENIC ROUTE →

Let kids make simple costumes and props for use during the presentation. Cut brown paper bags and turn them into tunics. Use bath tissue and paper towels as bandages.

Items to Pack:

Bibles, paper, pencils, a variety of markers, poster board, construction paper, scissors, glue sticks, staplers

ADVENTURES IN GROWING

(10 minutes)

Caring Ways

Kids will think of specific ways to care for others.

Say: ◖God wants us to care for others. And he wants us to care for everyone—not just our friends.

Form groups of four, and give each group a Bible. Set the supplies in the center of the room.

Say: **In your group, think how this parable could relate to your everyday life. Who is someone you might not normally consider a neighbor—and how could you care for that person? Then think of a way to present your idea to the rest of us.**

Maybe you'll think of someone like the bully at school, or the new kid in the neighborhood who doesn't dress like everyone else. Then think of a way to care for that person—maybe inviting the person to church, or even just smiling and saying hello to someone everyone else ignores.

Then choose supplies from the center of the room, and come up with a way to present your idea. Maybe you'll draw a picture or poster, make a comic book, create a skit to act out, write song—it's up to you! The only rule is that everyone in your group has to be involved. I'll give you about five minutes. Oh, and feel free to look up Luke 10:25-37 in your Bible for a refresher of the parable!

Offer help as needed. After five minutes or so, call time. Have each group present its idea, followed by a round of applause.

Say: **Thanks for those ideas!** ◖God wants us to care for others, **and you all seem to really understand what Jesus meant by this parable. I hope you'll follow through this week and care for someone you might not have thought of before. In fact, let's make sure that happens!**

SOUVENIRS

(10 minutes)

Caring Hands

Kids will see that they can care for others in a variety of ways.

Items to Pack:
a photocopy of the "Caring Hands" handout from page 117 for each child, pens, scissors, glue sticks

Set out supplies to share. Give each person a copy of the "Caring Hands" handout.

Say: **Today we're learning that God wants us to care for others. From the parable we heard, we know that God wants us to care for all kinds of people—not just our friends. Let's make something to help us remember to do just that.**

Have kids cut out both handprints on the page. Then have them line up the hand patterns and glue the edges together, leaving an opening at the wrists. Have kids write the following words on the fingers of their handprints:

- on the thumb write "home"
- on the pointer finger write "school"
- on the middle finger write "neighborhood"
- on the ring finger write "church"
- on the pinkie finger write "world"

TOUR GUIDE TIP

Help younger children cut out simple mitten shapes, rather than cutting out the individual fingers. Also help them write the words on the fingers.

Say: **Take your Caring Hands home with you in your Travel Journals today as reminders that God wants us to care for others. You can care for lots of people—from people in your family to people around the world! Use the words you wrote to help you think of others to care for. Each time you care for someone, write what you did on a scrap of paper, and place it inside your caring hands.**

Before we close, let's take a minute to thank God for teaching us how to care for others.

HOME AGAIN PRAYER

(10 minutes)

Use this experience to reinforce with kids that God wants them to care for others.

Items to Pack:
pens, adhesive bandages

Gather kids in a circle with you on the floor. Set pens in the center of the circle.

Say: **One way to care for others is to pray for them. Right now, think of someone you know who could use prayer. You won't have to say the person's name. When you've thought of someone, write the**

TOUR GUIDE TIP
Tell younger writers that they can each draw a small heart instead of writing a person's name.

person's name or initials in small letters on the back of your hand. Pause as kids write.

The Samaritan in our parable wrapped the hurt man in bandages. I'm going to give each of you a bandage. Unwrap it and place it over the name you wrote on your hand. Help kids as needed. Then collect and dispose of the trash.

Pray: **God, thank you for sending Jesus to teach us how to care for others. Thank you for caring for us with your great love. This week, help us to be like the good Samaritan who went out of his way to care for the poor traveler. Please help us to pray for and care for the people we thought of. In Jesus' name, amen.**

Make sure all kids take home their Travel Journals and thank them for journeying with you through the parables of Jesus.

Mouth-Watering Bread Recipe

Because an oven and a knife are involved, you need a parent to help you with this recipe. But that's okay—you'll be proud to share the loaf of tasty wonderfulness you bake! While you're making the bread, tell your parent about Jesus' Parable of the Yeast (Matthew 13:33) and what you've learned about how God's kingdom grows.

You'll need this much time:

About 3 hours to prepare the bread

45 minutes for the bread to bake

You'll need these ingredients:

¾ cup warm (not hot!) water

1 package active dry yeast

1 teaspoon salt

1½ teaspoons of sugar

1 tablespoon (note: this is a slightly bigger spoon!) vegetable shortening

½ cup of milk

3 cups all-purpose flour (though you may not use all of it)

1-2 tablespoons butter

(optional) raisins, brown sugar, and cinnamon, if you'd like to make cinnamon bread

Simple Steps:

1. Put the water in a large bowl and slowly stir in the yeast until the yeast dissolves.

2. Add the sugar, salt, shortening, and milk to the bowl. Gently stir it all together.

3. Mix in the first cup of flour, and then the second.

4. Decide: Do you need more flour? The dough should be slightly sticky, but be stiffening as you mix it. If you need more flour—and you might—add a tablespoon at a time.

5. Put the dough on a floured bread board and knead it. Add small amounts of flour until the dough is soft, smooth, and isn't sticky.

6. Toss in a handful of raisins, a pinch of brown sugar, and a sprinkling of cinnamon if you want to do so.

7. Place the dough in a bowl that's been buttered so the bread won't stick. Flip the bread over so the top is glazed with butter. Sprinkle on more cinnamon.

8. Cover the dough with a cotton (non-fuzzy!) towel and place in a warm spot.

9. Wait an hour. Let the yeast do its stuff.

10. Come back and punch down the dough as you stick it back on the floured board. Knead the dough again as an oven preheats to 375 degrees F.

11. You did involve an adult, right? Because 375 degrees is *really* hot.

12. Form the dough into a loaf and set it into a buttered bread pan.

13. Cover the dough and let it rise for a half hour.

14. Oops...guess you could have waited to preheat the oven but you'll know better next time.

15. With a sharp knife (adult help again) cut three slashes across the top of the loaf. Place the loaf in the oven.

16. Let bake for about 40 minutes or until the kitchen smells wonderful and the loaf is a perfect golden brown.

17. Remove the loaf from the bread pan and let it cool on a clean dishtowel.

18. Bask in glory when you share it with your family. You're a legend!

Kids' Travel Guide™ Series

Kids' Travel Guide to the Armor of God

The world is a scary place, but God is greater than it all! This edition of the *Kids' Travel Guide* series leads your Sunday school or midweek program on a 13-week Scripture-based exploration of the armor of God. Lead them to have a faith so bold they'll be able to stand firm in the midst of terrifying or unclear situations. Kids (levels K-5th grade) will explore how to be strong in the decisions they make, and in relationships with others. *Kids' Travel Guide™ to the Armor of God* is perfect for helping children learn about spiritual issues in a non-threatening and empowering way. **Flexible**—works for 2 kids…12 kids…20 kids!

▶ ISBN 978-0-7644-2695-7 • $19.99

Kids' Travel Guide to the 23rd Psalm
▶ ISBN 978-0-7644-4005-2
$19.99

Kids' Travel Guide to the Fruit of the Spirit
▶ ISBN 978-0-7644-2390-1
$19.99

Kids' Travel Guide to the Lord's Prayer
▶ ISBN 978-0-7644-2524-0
$19.99

Kids' Travel Guide to the Ten Commandments
▶ ISBN 978-0-7644-2224-9
$19.99

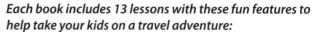

Each book includes 13 lessons with these fun features to help take your kids on a travel adventure:

- **In-Focus Verse** around which the adventure is focused.
- **Departure Prayer** designed for children to add their own words of prayer.
- **First-Stop Discoveries:** Narrated enactment or group activity exploring the lesson's Bible story.
- **Story Excursions:** Through Bible stories, bring the book's biblical theme to life in fun, imaginative, and dramatic ways.
- **Adventures in Growing:** Activities show kids how to apply what they've learned to their daily lives!
- **Souvenirs:** Kids create pages that go into a notebook (their very own travel journal!) to remind them of the lesson's Bible point.